HISTORIC CORBRIDGE

its streets and buildings

DAVID WAUGH

CORBRIDGE VILLAGE TRUST

HISTORIC CORBRIDGE

CONTENTS

There is a fold-out map on the inside of the front cover which is number referenced to specific buildings and other features mentioned in the text.

The illustration featured on the front and back cover is the village tithe map of 1780.

BIBLIOGRAPHY

Readers are referred to to the following publications for further information regarding the history of Corbridge:

History of Corbridge
Robert Forster (1881)

Comprehensive Guide to Northumberland
W.W. Tomlinson (1888)

Corbridge: The Saxon Royal Town.
S.F. Dixon (1912)

A History of Northumberland. Vol X. 'Corbridge'
H.H.E. Craster (1914)

Corbridge, Border Village
Walter Iley (1974)

The Buildings of England: Northumberland.
Nikolaus Pevsner (1992)

Corbridge, The last two thousand years
Gillian Dickinson (2000)

Parish Council web site **www.corbridge.gov.uk**

ACKNOWLEDGEMENTS

Members of the Village Trust committee:
Michael Cunliffe, Richard Hart-Jackson, David Hubbick, Albert Knight, Peter Lucas, Gilbert Marshall, David Nicol, Michael Rae, Susan Ramsay and David Waugh.

Residents who have donated their time, knowledge and materials:
Sir Lawrie Barratt, John Bishop, Muriel and Alan Bowman, Marcus and Paul Davison, Bob Douglas, John Graham, George Hall, John Joyce and family, Pip Moon, Neville Rutherford, Jennie and David Thompson, Roger Tillotson, David Walters and Janet Wormold.

Original and archive photographs:
Cover photograph: Dae Sasitorn, Lastrefuge.co.uk.
Peter Atkinson, inside front-cover and pages 20-21.
Donna Barkess, pages 4-5, 7, 10-15, 17-19, 23, 26-39, 41, 43-44, 46-47. Sir Lawrie Barratt, page 40. Corbridge Village Trust archives, pages 6, 16, 24, 36. Bob Douglas, pages 22, 25, 27, 32, 34, 37, 42. English Heritage, page 4. George Hall, pages 15, 29, 46. Hexham Courant, page 47. Iain Kerr, inside front-cover and pages 3, 23. Peter Lucas, pages 6, 19, 21, 25, 41-42, 45. Seth Tinsley, page 25. Stuart Twist, page 17. David Waugh, pages 44-45. Corbridge Official Guide, title page. H.H.E. Craster: A History of Northumberland, pages 5-6, 9, 26. W.J. Palmer: The Tyne and its Tributaries, p 45.

Editor:
Katherine James.

Design and artwork:
© Iain Kerr Associates, www.iainkerrassociates.co.uk

Published by:
David Waugh © 2007
ISBN 978-0-9557809-0-5

FOREWORD

Since Corbridge Village Trust was formed back in 1965, our aims have been to preserve and promote the distinctive and delightful characteristics of our village, for the mutual benefit of local residents and also our many welcome visitors. To this end we are delighted to have contributed to the research and local knowledge that has culminated in this book *'Historic Corbridge, its streets and buildings'*.

Taking as his starting point the very successful Village Trust publication *'A Walk of Discovery'*, David Waugh has produced this informative and enjoyable meander through the streets of Corbridge. Along the way the history, architecture, and some of the colourful characters of the village, are brought to life. We are sure that everyone; be they residents, former villagers, tourists or social historians, will find something to fascinate and interest them within its pages.

Of course, any book of this nature cannot be definitive and comprehensive in every respect, as the village continues to develop and new archaeological discoveries come to light. David Waugh and the Village Trust will welcome any further research, anecdotes, pictures and recollections from readers that might help to expand the historical archive of Corbridge for future publications.

Corbridge Village Trust

AN INTRODUCTION BY THE AUTHOR.

As a geographer, who has spent most of his working life teaching this fascinating subject, I have always been interested in the location of settlements and their subsequent development and change. It is evident that Corbridge, as with any village of antiquity, has a wealth of social, architectural and historical stories built into virtually every street and alleyway and so I was delighted to take on the task of writing this book, at the request of the Village Trust.

Having written over fifty geography text books for 11 to 18 year olds, I have always aimed to produce works which are accurate, accessible, attractive and, of course, informative. I hope you will find that *'Historic Corbridge'* is no exception to this rule! Whether you use it as a guidebook, as you explore the village, or peruse it at your leisure at home, I trust you will find it as enjoyable to read as I did to write.

David Waugh

The Romans
AD 70 to 400

The Romans chose this site at a strategic crossing point over the Tyne and at the intersection of two important roads – Dere Street (running north–south) and Stanegate (linking the east–west forts along the Tyne Valley). These roads, the Roman legacy to Corbridge, remained in use for over a thousand years. Corstopitum, as it was called, was initially a timber-built fort set up as a base for horses and supplies and was about half a mile west of the present-day village. After this and two successive timber-built forts had been destroyed by the Scots, a mainly stone-built fort was built c.AD 140 when the Romans tried to re-occupy Scotland. Within twenty years they had retreated, reducing the military importance of Corstopitum which then became mainly a civilian settlement, the most northerly town in their Empire, with tradesmen and merchants. It remained in use until about AD 400 after which it fell into permanent decay.

Date	Significant Events
AD 79	The Romans arrive under Agricola. Site chosen for a bridge over the Tyne.
81	Romans establish a timber fort and supply station at Corstopitum (Coria).
c.140	Roman fort rebuilt mainly in stone.
c.160	Becomes a civilian rather than a military settlement.
c.400	Romans have left Corstopitum.

The Corbridge Lion.

Angles, Saxons, Vikings and Danes
650 to 1066

Little is known for the next three centuries except that a new village, the present-day Corbridge, was founded half a mile downriver from the abandoned Roman bridge and adjacent to an excellent site for a ford. It seems that by 771 there was a monastery church where, in 786, the Bishop of Mayo was consecrated. Corbridge was one of the earliest of Anglian settlements in northern England and it became a centre for their administration. Later, in Saxon times, it became a royal burh (town) and some believe that, for a short period, it replaced Bamburgh as the capital of Northumbria. It came under increasing attack from the Danes who won important local battles in 796 and 918.

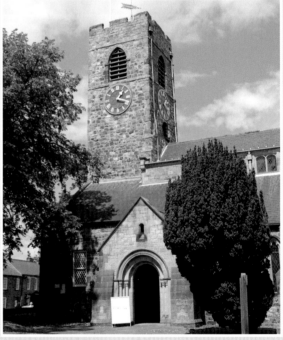

The Saxon church tower.

Date	Significant Events
674–680	Likely foundation of the church, or monastery, of St Andrew's. Et Corabrige (the Anglian name) grows steadily in size and importance.
771	Evidence of a thriving monastery.
786	Consecration of Aldulf, Bishop of Mayo (Ireland) in St Andrew's Church.
796	Ethelred, King of Northumbria, killed at the Battle of Corbridge (Corebrygge).
918	Danes defeat armies of Northumbria and Scotland at Corbridge.
923	Monastery believed to have been destroyed by the Danes.

Romans (70AD to 400) Angles, Saxons, Vikings & Danes (650 to 1066) Normans (1066 to 1295) Middle Ages & Tudors (1296 to 1603) 17th C. 18th C. 19th C. 20th C.

100   200   300   400   500   600   700   800   900   1000   1100   1200   1300   1400   1500   1600   1700   1800   1900   2000

The Normans and early Plantagenets
1066 to 1295

The Vicar's Pele.

This became a 'golden age' for Corbridge. The settlement grew in size and wealth and by the end of the 13th century it was second in importance only to Newcastle in the county. Three years after King John's visit in 1201, when Corbridge was granted the privilege of farming its own land, the first Stagshaw Fair was held (page 20). A new bridge across the Tyne in 1235 led to an increase in trade, there was a weekly market and the village had its own common seal. This greater prosperity resulted in St Andrew's Church being enlarged to four times its former size (page 18) and the building of three sister churches: St Helen's, Trinity and St Mary's. In 1295 Corbridge sent two burgesses (Adam son of Alan and Hugh son of Hugh) to the first English Parliament although this, for financial reasons, was never repeated; while the population of about 1,500 would not be reached again for another 600 years (page 8).

Date	Significant Events
1095	Tithes paid to the Priory at Tynemouth.
1128	St Andrew's Church passes to the Canons of Carlisle.
1138	King David I of Scotland occupies Corbridge.
1195	Record of a vicarage being built. Oldest parts of Low Hall built.
1201	King John visits Corbridge granting it a charter, allows a weekly market and orders a 'dig' at Corstopitum for treasure (none is found).
1204	First Stagshaw Fair.
1235	The first Corbridge Ancient Common Seal with the legend '+ Sigill Commune Corebrigie'. Medieval bridge built to west of present bridge.
1278	The Manor of Corbridge reverts to the Crown.
1295	Two burgesses sent to the first English Parliament (Edward I's Model Parliament). Population is about 1,500 – second largest in the county after Newcastle
1296	Bridge, churches and houses destroyed by Scots under William Wallace. Edward I gives gift of 40 oaks to rebuild burnt houses (nothing for the bridge).

The Middle Ages and Tudors
1296 to 1603

Two events were to end this prosperity. The first was the Scottish wars which led, initially, to the destruction of the village in 1296. On this occasion three of the four churches were destroyed (never to be rebuilt), as was the bridge over the river, while the timber-framed and thatched houses were burnt to the ground. The village was to be sacked twice again by the Scots, in 1312 and 1346, watched, perhaps, by the Vicar safe in his stone Pele House built early in the 14th century (page 19). The second event was the Black Death of 1349 which, it is estimated, killed over half of Corbridge's population. The village, with its street pattern the same as it is today although the names have changed (page 9), remained in poverty during the Wars of the Roses and in Tudor times – a period also of the Border Reivers.

Date	Significant Events
1300	The manor hall of Hallgarth built on Hall Walls (now The Chains).
1306	Edward I stays for three nights.
1310	King's Oven first used for the communal baking of bread and meat.
c.1310	Pele Tower built as the vicar's residence.
1312	Sacked by Scots under Robert the Bruce.
1332	Edward III grants Manor of Corbridge to Henry, Earl of Northumberland.
1346	Village sacked by Scots under David II; stragglers from this army return after being massacred at Neville's Cross.
1349	Black Death kills over half the population.
1536	Percy family lose the Manor of Corbridge after they support the Pilgrimage of Grace.
1578	Record of a parish school.

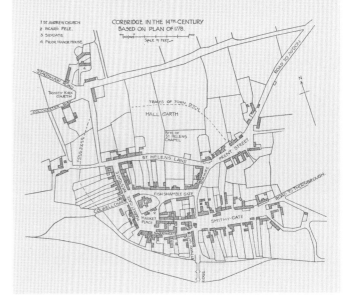

The 17th Century

The Act of Union, when the English and Scottish crowns were joined, at last restored peace in the region – apart from in 1644 when, during the Civil War, a band of Scots was routed just outside the village by English-Royalist forces. Despite the presence of several large estates around Corbridge, most of the village itself remained poor. However, there was evidence of some increase in wealth as indicated by stone being used instead of timber for some houses (such as Monks Holme) although most still had their thatched roofs. Travel was also made easier by the building of the present bridge in 1674 and the development of turnpike roads.

Monks Holme.

Date	Significant Events
c.1640	Monks Holme built.
1640	Corbridge loyal to the King during Civil War.
1644	Royalists fight the Scots in a skirmish just west of the village.
1674	Present bridge over River Tyne built.
1695	Date on a lintel behind the Wheatsheaf.

The bridge over the Tyne.

The 18th Century

The Black Bull, photographed in 1950.

Apart from some new buildings, such as the Golden Lion, that used stones from nearby Dilston Hall, the village seems to have been little affected by the active support for the Stuarts by the Radcliffe family, and by the 3rd Earl of Derwentwater in particular, during the Jacobite uprisings of 1715 and 1745. This century saw the erection of many of the older buildings that can still be seen in the streets leading from the Market Place. Most of these buildings were, and remain, of good quality. There was also the development of several trades linked to farming and farm products (page 16). Hutchinson, however, said on a visit in 1766 that while Corbridge looked a pleasant place, it was in reality 'dirty and disagreeable' (page 8).

Date	Significant Events
1707	Oswald Cottage built in Front Street.
1715	First Jacobite uprising (supported by 3rd Earl of Derwentwater of Dilston Castle).
1734	Corbridge Lanx, a Roman silver dish, found in river bank – now in British Museum.
1745	Second Jacobite uprising.
1755	Usher House (now the Black Bull) built and the 'Old' Bluebell Inn opens.
1756	Cross House built.
1750s	Aydon Road built to connect Corbridge with the new Military Road.
1767	Workhouse opens and church clock ordered.
1768	Golden Lion built using stones from Dilston Hall.
1770	Heron House built.
1771	Only bridge to survive the Tyne flood.
1776	Enclosure Act creates fields in and around Corbridge.

Romans (70AD to 400) Angles, Saxons, Vikings & Danes (650 to 1066) Normans (1066 to 1295) Middle Ages & Tudors (1296 to 1603) 17th C. 18th C. 19th C. 20th C.

100 200 300 400 500 600 700 800 900 1000 1100 1200 1300 1400 1500 1600 1700 1800 1900 2000

The 19th Century

Despite an increase in the types and range of cottage industries (page 16), the living conditions in Corbridge were, like most other places in Britain, extremely poor. Although MacKenzie said in 1825 that people came here because 'they were out of health', in 1830 the historian Hodgson described the town as being 'filthy with middens and pigsties' (page 8). The coming of the railway in 1838 led to an increase in population, trade and wealth and by 1880, when sanitary conditions had also improved, the village was described as 'being well-built on the north bank of the Tyne and with gardens dipping gently into the river'.

Date	Significant Events
1801	First census gives population as 1,032.
1814	Percy Cross erected in Market Place.
1815	Pant erected in Market Place.
1821	Population of 1,254 (613 males; 641 females) living in 230 houses.
1822	Of 37 deaths, 18 are aged over 60 (1 is 99, 1 is 100).
1828	Corbridge has eight inns.
1835	Newcastle to Hexham railway opens (1838 to Carlisle).
1840	Bottle kilns of the Corbridge Pottery built.
1847	Stone from Piper's Cross Quarry used for Newcastle's High Level Bridge.
1849	Duke of Northumberland grants 74 allotments on The Chains.
1851	Population rises to 1,363.
1855	Church of England school opens.
1861	Robert Forster adds minute-hand to church clock.
1863	Gas first used in houses and for street lamps.
1864	Methodist Church built at junction of Hill Street and Princes Street.
1872	New cemetery opens replacing St Andrew's Churchyard.
1881	River bridge widened by 3 feet.
1884	First supply of water to some houses.
1887	Town Hall built.
1888	New bells for St Andrew's Church.
1895	First meeting of the Parish Council.
1897	New church clock for Queen Victoria's Jubilee.

The 20th Century

This century saw a rapid transformation, mainly resulting from the increase in the number of cars and buses, the improvements in roads and the change of the village into both a commuter settlement and a place for retirement. Most of the 19th century trades disappeared and were replaced by continual improvements in the quality of housing and services, making Corbridge a highly desirable place in which to live and, by the introduction of specialist shops and quality eating and drinking places, making it attractive for day visitors.

Date	Significant Events
1901	Post Office moves from Front Street to Main Street (later to Hill Street).
1906	First organised archaeological excavations at Corstopitum.
1907	The Corbridge Lion found at Corstopitum – now in the local museum.
1908	Northumberland County Council opens Corbridge School.
1909	Lloyds Bank opens.
1918	Charlotte Straker Hospital opens. Corbridge WI founded.
1920	Barclays Bank opens in Market Place.
1922	Parish Hall built.
1930	Last Stagshaw Fair.
1943–58	Cinema at rear of Town Hall.
1947	Jean Hickleton takes over ladies clothes shop in Middle Street (became 'Norma James' in 1970).
1951	Population is 2,434.
1955	Worst river flood since 1881.
1962	Electricity replaces gas for street lighting.
1965	Corbridge Village Trust founded.
1970s	Catherine Cookson lives at Town Barns.
1974	Corbridge first designated a Conservation Area.
1976	Library opens in former Methodist Church.
1976	A69 by-pass opens.
1987	Fred Dibnah lowers the chimney at Jameson's pottery and brickworks.
1992	Opening of Charlotte Straker Care Centre.
1995	Saxon waterwheel excavated.
1996	Conservation Area extended.
1997	Post Office moves from Hill Street to Town Hall buildings.

The Market Place Cross

VILLAGE DESCRIPTIONS

Places, and how different people see them, change over time. This may be seen in the following personal descriptions of Corbridge.

King John 1201

He caused a search to be made at Corbridge "imagining that the town had once been large and populous, and must have been ruined by an earthquake, or some sudden and terrible invasion, and that in either case the people would have been unable to remove their wealth." Tradition says the search was in vain.

Morden about 1700

"… there is nothing remarkable in this town but the Church and a little tower-house, inhabited by the Vicars of the place, yet there are so many remains of ancient buildings as prove it to have been a large and spacious town."

Hutchinson 1766

"Though the town makes a pretty appearance at the foot of the vale when you see it from Hexham, it disappoints the traveller greatly on his entrance to find it dirty and disagreeable."

MacKenzie 1825

"Corbridge is esteemed a peculiarly healthy place, and of late has been much frequented by persons out of health. It is divided into eight streets which by the returns in 1821 comprised 231 houses which are occupied by 1254 inhabitants."

Hodgson 1830

"The town (for such its antiquity demands that it be styled) is dirty, and in all the streets except that through which the Newcastle and Carlisle road passes, filthy with middens and pigsties, with railing before them of split board, etc."

Forster 1881

"The absence of all manufactures or anything causing injury to health, the situation of the village, its fine springs of water, its health-giving breezes, its pleasant walks, its nearness to the railway station, all contribute to make it a delightful and enticing resort for visitors in quest of recreation, entertainment or health."

Tomlinson 1888

Corbridge is "one of the most picturesque and interesting of Northumbrian villages, as it is one of the most considerable. From its high and dry situation on a gravelly hill, which is sheltered on the north and south by the steep sides of the river gorge, combined with the loveliness of the surrounding country, Corbridge has become one of the most popular health resorts in the county. Few villages, indeed, have so many natural advantages, and these are supplemented by historic associations of exceptional interest."

Iley 1970

"Corbridge today is eminently satisfactory. It is far from perfection, and would not, I think, win any prizes in 'Best' or 'Tidiest' villages competitions: it would not, in any event, dream of entering for them. It is in many ways a workaday village, with highly competitive pubs and restaurants, and busy shops. It is by no means lost in a dream of its own loveliness, as some villages seem; when people come here they do not say 'Isn't it lovely?', and tiptoe quietly away: they go shopping, or seek what suits them best for food and drink and company."

Village Trust 2007

"The village has been transformed into both a commuter settlement and a place for retirement. Continual improvements in the quality of housing and services have made Corbridge a highly desirable, but expensive, place in which to live while the introduction of specialist shops and the quality of eating and drinking places have made it attractive for day visitors."

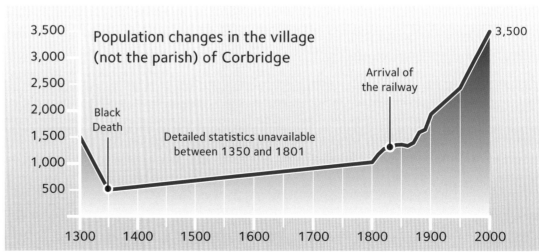

Population changes in the village (not the parish) of Corbridge

Street names in use in
the 14th century.

St. HELEN'S LANE

PRENT STREET

WESTGATE

GORMIRE

FISH SHAMBLE GATE

EASTGATE

COLWELL
CHARE

THE DRIFT

MARKET
GATE

MARKET
PLACE

SIDGATE

SMITHYGATE

NARROWGATE

St. MARY'S
GATE

Position of Bridge
(not in use)

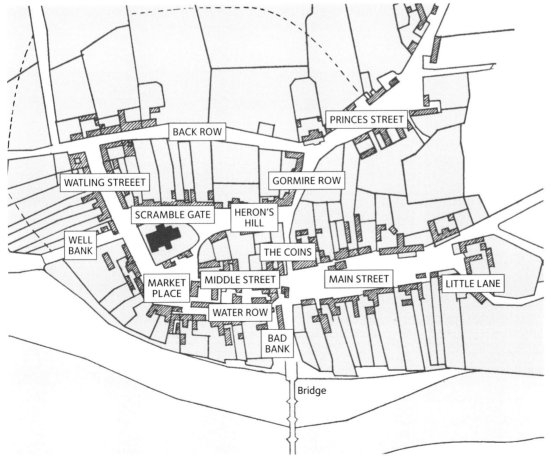

Street names in use in 1863.

BACK ROW

PRINCES STREET

WATLING STREEET

GORMIRE ROW

SCRAMBLE GATE

HERON'S
HILL

WELL
BANK

THE COINS

MARKET
PLACE

MIDDLE STREET

MAIN STREET

LITTLE LANE

WATER ROW

BAD
BANK

Bridge

VILLAGE ARCHITECTURE

During the Middle Ages, and up to the 18th century, most houses in Corbridge would probably have had a timber frame, daub and wattle walls and a thatched, usually of heather, roof – materials easily collected and used and just as easily burnt during the Scottish Wars and by Border Reivers. Windows would be openings without glass and a hole in the roof would serve as a chimney. The exceptions were the stone-built pele tower-houses of the **Vicar's Pele** (page 19) and Low Hall (page 38). **Low Hall** and, from Jacobean times, **Monks Holme** (page 39), also had **mullion** windows and decorated **finials**.

By the late 17th and early 18th centuries ordinary houses were built of stone, several of which still survive in terraces in the streets leading from the Market Place. By the middle of the 19th century slate increasingly began to replace thatch as the main roofing material. The 1841 census names John Smith, aged 70, of Water Row, as being a thatcher and Robert Kirtley, aged 75, of Watling Street, as a slater.

By the middle of the 19th century, partly as an indication of growing wealth, houses became more elaborate. Walls were built with **ashlar** stone blocks rather than **random dressed rubble**, while decorated **quoins** were added around doors and windows as well as marking the end of a terrace. Brick-built houses, such as **Gresham House**, were the exception. Forster, writing in 1881, claimed that in the previous thirty years one-fifth of the houses had either been rebuilt or were new.

As in all settlements, some residents were more wealthy than others and, as a result, built larger and more elaborate houses. In Corbridge these are seen in Hill Street with Heron House and the properties immediately adjacent to it (page 32). Heron House has an ornate doorway with moulded **architraves** and a decorated **pediment** while the houses next to it to the east have **oriel** windows, supported by **corbels**, and a **string course**. Several houses in Front Street have **gables** with decorated finials. It is only in Main Street (pages 36 to 41) that large, detached houses can be found but even here building styles and materials match those of the remainder of central Corbridge.

Changes over time
Most buildings have features, however small, that make them different to other buildings. Bearing in mind the limitations of making generalisations and in creating stereotypes, it is possible to simplify some of these features to show how, in the case of Corbridge, they have changed over a period of time.

Period	Walls	Windows	Doors	Roof
Middle Ages to late 17th C.	Timber	Mullion or open	Timber lintel	Thatch (heather)
18th C.	Uncoursed rubble	Stone lintels and sills. Sash	Stone lintel	Thatch or slate
Early 19th C.	Random dressed rubble	Stone lintels and sills. Sash	Stone lintels and dressed quoins	Thatch or slate
Late 19th C.	Ashlar masonry	Stone lintels and sills with dressed quoins	Stone lintels and dressed quoins	Slate
Larger Houses	Ashlar masonry	Dressed quoins. Oriels on corbels	Decorative architraves and pediments	Slate. Finials

Ⓐ Low Hall

B

Finial (B) – an ornamental topmost feature above a gable, e.g. Narrowgate House, Monks Holme, Eastgate House.

C

Lintel (C) – a horizontal beam of wood or stone bridging an opening, notably a window or a door.

D

Sash (D) – an 18th century invention to improve ventilation by sliding a window up or down to allow air to enter.

Mullion window (A) – a vertical bar, traditionally stone, dividing panes of glass, e.g. 32 Hill Street, Low Hall, Monks Holme.

Rubble (C) – uncoursed or random dressed material used for outside walls of older buildings, e.g. 21-27 Middle Street, 6-8 Watling Street.

Sill (C) – a horizontal structure beneath a window to protect the underlying wall, especially if made with random rubble, from damp.

VILLAGE ARCHITECTURE

Gable (E) – a triangular shaped section of wall at the end of a building or a row houses e.g. Heron House, Low Hall.

Quoins (E) - dressed stones at the corner of a building or around a doorway or window, e.g. Wheatsheaf Inn, 6-8 Watling Street, 14-16 Front Street. Also known as 'long and short work'.

Oriel (H) - A window projecting from the wall of a house at an upper level, usually resting on corbels, e.g. 14-16 Hill Street, Town Hall building.

Double fronted (E) - a house with a central front door and windows to either side e.g. Corbridge House, Riverhill.

Ashlar (F) - masonry of large square cut stones, e.g. Golden Lion, Glenthorne.

Date and for whom built (G) e.g. Heron House, Oswald Cottage.

String course (G) – a horizontal course of stone across a house mainly for decoration but can help support an upper storey, e.g. Heron House, 14-16 Hill Street.

Dormer window (B) – a window projecting from the slope of a roof and having a roof of its own e.g. 14 Hill Street, Laurel House.

Voussoir (H) – a wedged-shape stone that forms part of an arch, the central one being known as the keystone, e.g. west end of St Andrew's Church, Town Hall building.

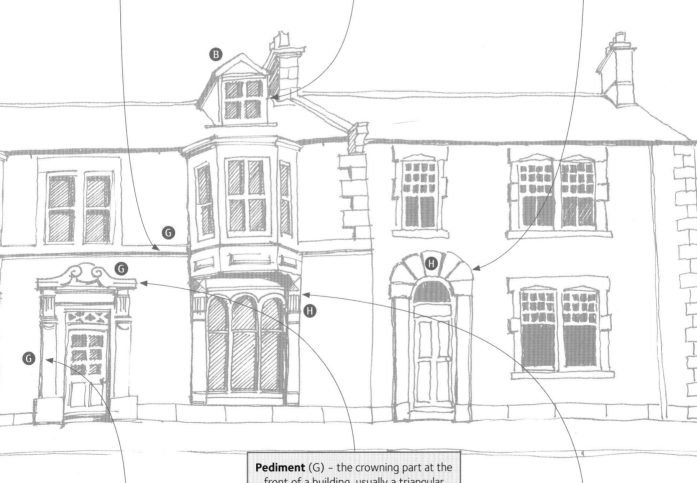

Architrave (G) - a moulded frame, often decorated, around a doorway or window (also shouldered architrave), e.g. Heron House.

Pediment (G) - the crowning part at the front of a building, usually a triangular shape located above door, e.g. Black Bull, Wheatsheaf Inn, Cross House. A **swan's neck pediment** is curved and may include rosettes, e.g. Dunedin, Heron House.

Corbel (H) –a projecting block of stone or timber supporting something above it, e.g. 14-16 Hill Street, Town Hall building.

VILLAGE WATER SUPPLY

The Roman camp at **Corstopitum** had its own water supply. An aqueduct or conduit, dating from about AD 180, brought water from the nearby Cor Burn to the fountain house which was located on Stanegate, the main street. The water was then discharged through an ornamental spout into a large aeration cistern where it was allowed to mix with the air to restore its freshness. From here it flowed into a huge stone tank, located outside, from which it could be taken for everyday public use.

Medieval Corbridge had two main sources of water – the spring in Carr's Field and St Andrew's Well.

Carr's Field, now a housing development with the same name, was at the eastern end of the village. From the early 13th century, and possibly even from Anglo-Saxon times, water from here was piped to the Market Place. This pipe fell into disuse and was forgotten for over 600 years until it was re-discovered in 1836 when trenches for a new drainage system were being dug. The old system consisted of lengths of ancient 2-inch bore lead pipes, in 2-foot lengths and strapped at their joints. The original pipe led in front of Low Hall and along the north side of Main and Middle Streets. During this time, a second pipe was added to take water from Carr's Field down to what was then the 'Drift' or 'Drove Road' and is now the pant on Spoutwell Lane (presumably for cattle crossing the nearby ford, page 39). This pant still proves to be a reliable source of water, maintaining a good flow even during times of drought.

St Andrew's Well, located on Well Bank (page 24), provided water for people living in the western part of the village. There has been no remaining evidence of this well since 1992 when the area was filled in.

The **Princes Street** or **Birch's Pant** was erected in the 1760s by Eliezer Birch (page 30). This, the first pant or drinking fountain in the village, still issues water. It proved a useful watering place for draft horses that drew carriages as it was near to the Toll House and was just before the steep pull up to Aydon and the then new Military Road.

The **Market Place** and **Main Street Pants** were both erected in the early 19th century. That in the Market Place was given, as the plaque on it records (page 20), by Hugh Percy, Duke of Northumberland in 1815. The Main Street Pant, paid for by public subscription, was erected in 1818 (page 41). The water for both pants came from the spring in Carr's Field. They are now ornamental features, their troughs filled with flowers.

Two other pants can still be seen. One is opposite the Wheatsheaf Inn and is ornamental, the other is on the Stagshaw Road just north of St Helen's Lane and provides a trickle of water.

At a meeting held in the Angel Inn in 1884, it was decided to borrow £2,000 so that water could be transferred from the Shaw Well (which is adjacent to the A68 about one mile north of the village) to those properties whose owners were prepared to pay for it. Following the passing of the 1944 Water Supplies and Sewerage Act, £60,000 was spent providing the village with a clean and reliable supply from the Shaw Well.

Today's supply is provided by Northumbrian Water Ltd. Water from the Hallington, Colt Crag and Catcleugh reservoirs is transferred to a large modern treatment works at Whittle Dene some 6 miles (10km) east of Corbridge. It is then piped to the village either under the Aydon Road or via the Shaw Well tank. Sewage is conveyed by gravity towards Well Green (page 24) where it is piped under the Tyne to a pumping station next to the flood-bank and on to the treatment works at Riding Mill. The treated effluent is then discharged into the river.

The Spout Well.

The Market Place Pant.

VILLAGE INNS, HOTELS & PUBLIC HOUSES

Corbridge had eight 'Hotels & Public Houses' listed in the 1827 edition of the *Parson & White Directory of Durham and Northumberland* and eight 'Hotels, Inns and Taverns', though not all the same, named in the 1886 edition of *Bulmer's History, Topography and Directory of Northumberland*. Today there are six surviving, as shown in the table below.

During the 19th century the village also had its own brewery located in present-day Springfield Mews (behind Low Hall).

Top: The Angel Inn, c.1880.

Above, from left:
The Golden Lion, The Dyvels and The Blue Bell.

Map Location	Name and/or former name of hostelry	Date		
		1827	1886	2007
37	**The Angel Inn** (Main Street page 36) is the oldest with a date of 1726.	🍺	🍺	🍺
34	**The Black Bull** (Middle Street page 35), despite a date of 1755 above a doorway, only became a public house some time between 1827 and 1886.		🍺	🍺
29	**The Blue Bell** (formerly Scramblegate, now Hill Street page 33) used to be known as **The New Blue Bell**	🍺	🍺	🍺
	The Boot and Shoe (formerly in Water Row, now Front Street page 43) became the original Ramblers and is still a restaurant.	🍺		
	The Golden Fleece (Princes Street page 31) of 1827 was, presumably, **The Beerhouse** of 1886. It is now a domestic dwelling.	🍺	🍺	
22	**The Golden Lion** (formerly Heron's Hill, now Hill Street page 33) was built in the late 1760s	🍺	🍺	🍺
	The New Inn (Main Street), now the present–day Monks Holme (page 39), was used as a public house between 1827 and 1890.	🍺		
	The Old Bluebell Inn (Market Place page 21) was pulled down in 1890 and replaced by the **Tynedale Hotel** which in turn has closed.	🍺	🍺	
13	**The Wheatsheaf** (Watling Street page 23) was a farm in the seventeenth century, before becoming a hotel.	🍺	🍺	🍺
64	**The Dyvels** (Station Road page 47), formerly known as **The Station Hotel**, was built in the 1840s after the opening of the railway.		🍺	🍺

Riddell's Shop, 1913.

VILLAGE TRADES AND OCCUPATIONS

Until the beginning of the last century, the late 13th century had been the most prosperous and populated era in the history of the village. King John, following his visit in 1201, allowed local people to farm their own land and to hold a weekly Saturday market. Trade, and the success of the annual Stagshaw Fair (page 20), benefited both from the ever-increasing flow through the village of travellers, traders, goods and driven farm stock and from a new bridge built over the Tyne in 1235. By the 1290s, Corbridge had a population of 1,500 (not exceeded until the 1881 census), four churches and two Members of Parliament. Those listed on the Subsidy Roll of 1296, a tax imposed by Edward I on the 77 trades-people living in Corbridge (only Newcastle in the county had more), included a weaver, miller, dyer, tailor, goldsmith, forester, shepherd, butcher and, surprisingly, a slater. Records from that date also refer to *'the shop on the south side of the churchyard where the goldsmiths live'*.

The 14th century saw a decline in wealth and population partly due to the beginning of three centuries of hostilities with the Scots which was perpetuated by the Border Reivers, and partly due to the Black Death which reached Corbridge in 1349. Little was recorded during the 15th and 16th centuries apart from the village becoming renowned for its iron-making skills (in the year 1525 alone four new forges were listed). Signs of an increase in prosperity only appeared with the stability that resulted from the peace with Scotland in 1603 and, later, the building of the bridge across the Tyne in 1674.

Before the Enclosure Act of 1776 land around the village was largely unproductive with inefficient strip farming providing the basis of agriculture.

1821 to 1841

Although in 1821 there were 16 shops and 8 inns, the village remained in a poor state (page 12). However, by the time the *Parson & White Directory of Durham and Northumberland* was published in 1827 and the 1841 census was taken, job opportunities had considerably improved. For example:

Market gardening was extremely important (the first Ordnance Survey map of 1863 shows that the village was still surrounded by orchards). Plums (the wood of the tree was ideal for making spinning wheels), apples, pears and gooseberries were grown and Corbridge was well-known for its potatoes and onions. The produce was loaded into panniers, put on horseback and taken to Newcastle – a four-hour walk in each direction!

Weaving was a major cottage industry with almost every household having a spinning wheel. These were needed to provide for the estimated 30 looms that were in continual use within the village. Also listed, both in the 1827 trades directory and the 1841 census, were dressmakers, tailors, seamstresses and drapers. Hats, bonnets and gloves were also made.

Shoemaking was another important trade with several manufacturers making shoes and wooden clogs. The clogs, which were lightweight and warm, were mainly for lead-miners and coal-miners. The so-called 'Shields shoes' were made for the fishermen of North Shields.

Seventeen **blacksmiths** were employed in six forges. Other jobs included stonemasons and builders; tilers, slaters and a thatcher; potters; cartwrights; a basketmaker and a brushmaker.

Lime-burning in and around the village was another important occupation.

In 1841, 50% of people employed were in primary activities, mainly agricultural labourers, 32% in manufacturing and 18% in the service sector (mostly domestic servants). The comparable figures for the whole of the UK in that year were 24%, 51% and 25%.

1871 to 1910

By the 1871 census there were 26 shops, several with splendid frontages that still exist today (page 34), and 8 inns (page 15).

The 1886 trades directory names 4 blacksmiths, 3 ironmongers, 5 shoemakers, 5 butchers, 7 draper/tailors, 2 confectioners and 1 each of a bookseller, fishmonger, greengrocer, hairdresser and newsagent.

By 1900 the weaving industry had died out but there were still several blacksmiths.

Walkers, who had located on Milkwell Lane about 1840 and who made sanitary ware, tiles and pipes, closed in 1910. Jameson's pottery and brickworks, located near a source of superior clay north of the village off the Aydon Road, opened in 1871. In 1900 it employed 40 people. Middlemiss, who built West Terrace, manufactured his bricks in West End Terrace (page 26). The 1896 OS map names a 'brickworks' in the station yard.

The number of orchards had declined due partly to the building of new houses and, even then, partly to the result of competition from foreign fruit.

Today

The last blacksmith, Charlie Knott, retired in the mid 1970s and the last shoemaker (cobbler), George Twist, in 1984. Jameson's pottery closed in 1986 (the site, developed by Wimpey's, is now a housing estate) leaving in the manufacturing sector within the village only a printer, a sign-writer, a furniture maker, a goldsmith and jeweller and an upholsterer. There are, however, many qualified builders, joiners, plumbers and decorators.

Residents are well provided with services that employ people in the post office, two banks, two estate agents, a solicitor's, the large new health centre, an osteopath, two dental practices, an optometrist, a veterinary practice, a kindergarten and two schools, a library, a nursing home and a residential care home. There are restaurants, cafés and six public houses as well as the butcher, baker, bookshop, grocer, fishmonger, chemist, florist, toyshop, delicatessen and shops selling fruit and vegetables, sweets, wine, hardware, sandwiches, art supplies, music, computers, tapestry and fabrics, a petrol station and a car body repair shop. For visitors there are many specialist, high-quality shops selling ladies and gentlemen's clothes, shoes, perfumes, antiques, paintings, jewellery, glassware and gifts.

It is the range in services and types of shop that makes Corbridge such an attractive place in which to live, work in or to visit.

Left: George Twist in his cobbler's workshop, 1984.

Below: Kilns in Milkwell Lane.

A programme for the 1887 production of 'The Messiah' by 60 voices of the Corbridge Choral Society included the following adverts:

E Robson	Clothing & bedding	Watling St. & Hill St.
M & C Robson	Confectioners	Middle Street
George Robson	Nurseryman & florist	Main Street
John Roddam	Butcher	Princes Street
Mathew Lee	Draper, shoes & grocer	Middle Street
M Martinson	Cabinet maker, joiner & ironmonger	Corbridge
Fairless Bros	Furnishing & ironmongers	Heron's Hill
Alexander Wade	Butcher	Heron's Hill
G McCall	Bookseller & stationer	Market Place
Heslop's	Grocery & provision stores	Market Place
Nicholas Richley	Tailor, hatter & mercer	Water Row

THE MARKET PLACE

This is the ancient centre of the village from where streets still radiate in their 13th and 14th century pattern. A 14th century map shows the Market Place extending north to present-day Well Bank and Hill Street and the whole area backed by buildings (page 9). In medieval times there were shops and booths against the churchyard wall. Most of the present-day buildings are well over 200 years old.

St Andrew's Church ❶ is the most prominent building. It was first mentioned in AD 786 when Adulf was consecrated Bishop of Mayo (Ireland) in what was referred to as *'the monastery at Corbridge'*. However, it may have been founded a century earlier when the priory church of Hexham was built. While part of the tower dates from Saxon times and an internal arch is Roman, most

of the present church is 13th century. Pevsner describes it as *'the most important surviving Saxon monument in Northumberland, except for Hexham crypt'*. Guidebooks are available in the church and voluntary guides are often there during the summer months. However, the guide does not refer to an event described in the Parochial Magazine of July 1897 which records how *'on 22nd June a new church clock, which had been subscribed for, was set in motion to mark Queen Victoria's Diamond Jubilee. The ceremony was performed by Mrs J.H. Straker of Howden Dene. It was preceded at 12.30 by lunch, for adults only, in the Town Hall. Children assembled in the Hipping Stone field at 2.30 to march, headed by the Corbridge Brass Band, to the Market Place to watch the proceedings. All this was followed by sports, for all ages, in the Hipping Stone field'*.

St Andrew's Church

The upper tower, with its louvre windows, is mainly 11th century using stones from Corstopitum. It was topped with an iron weather-vane in 1767. The lower part of the west tower was the original entrance to the Saxon church – probably pre-786. It has long since been blocked in but its voussoir stones (page 13) show worn crosses with diagonal limbs. There is a 12th century Norman doorway with a zig-zag (or chevron) moulding and inside is an original Roman arch. The lychgate was erected in 1919 as a First World War memorial.

The 'Roman' eagle.

The sundial on the south transept dates from 1694.

The original church clock was instigated in 1767 by Eliezer Birch who paid half the cost. It had two dials (faces) but only the hour hand. In 1861 Robert Forster added the minute hand (paid for by public subscription). The present mechanism dates from the 1897 Jubilee. On the north face is a stone, possibly part of a former Roman altar, showing an eagle with a hooked bill. The stained glass windows are all 1864 to 1975.

Roman arch, voussoir stones and the font.

St Andrew's **Churchyard** ❷ is a memorial to many generations of Corbridge citizens and families. The oldest legible gravestone is that of Nicholas Stokoe (1733) who lived in Westfield (page 41). Later additions include memorials to.

- John Jamieson who, in the 1840s, was the first resident to concern himself with the public health of the village

- Eliezer Birch who funded the workhouse, the first pant and the original church clock (page 30)

- Bartholomew Walker of Eastfield (page 37)

- Mr Lowery, a surgeon who built Riverhill (page 21).

The church cemetery closed in 1872 when the present one was opened across the river.

The Vicar's Pele ❸ stands to the south-east of the church. It was constructed as a fortified residence for the vicar with stones taken from Corstopitum. There is no evidence to support Forster's claim that at some time it was also used as a prison. A plaque reads *'This Pele tower, the finest of its kind, was built about 1300 for a Vicar of Corbridge and was lived in until the early 17th century'*. It then fell into disrepair before being restored in 1910 by the 7th Duke of Northumberland. It is now managed by the Parish Council and is available for ad hoc exhibitions and functions.

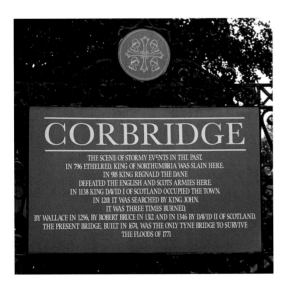

Next to the Vicar's Pele and on the footpath to Hill Street is a descriptive plaque (above) with, on one side, some important village dates and, on the other, a short account of Corbridge's history. Opposite is a chapel in Gothic style with slender arched windows, built in 1867 for the Primitive Methodists. In 1975 it merged with the Princes Street Church to form the Corbridge Methodist Church.

The Vicar's Pele

The three-storey tower is 30 feet high (almost 10 metres) with walls made from Roman-worked stones (sandstone) from Corstopitum which are over 4 feet thick.
- The upper storey was mainly for defence. It has loops (arrow slits) on three sides, probably for firing missiles.
- The middle floor was the living area with a fireplace, chimney-breast, two trefoil-headed windows with seats at their sides, a sink and access to a latrine.
- The lower floor was a vaulted basement where cattle were likely to have been kept at times of unrest. Its loops were probably to let in light and air.

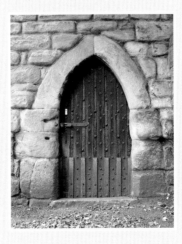

The original oak door covered with an iron grate.

Each corner has a corbel – a projecting bracket supporting other stones. The corbels are turreted and have narrow slits for the dropping or firing of missiles.

THE MARKET PLACE

The Market Cross **4** dominates the centre of the Market Place. The original cross was set up in the 13th century when Corbridge was the largest town in Northumberland after Newcastle. Its base was a worn circular stone probably taken from a Roman altar at Corstopitum. The cross was taken down in 1807 and replaced, in 1814, by the present cast-iron cross provided by the Lord of the Manor, the Duke of Northumberland, with the inscription *'HUGH PERCY DUKE OF NORTHUMBERLAND ANNO MDCCCXIIII'*. This cross, with the Duke's emblem of the Percy lion on the base, is also known as 'The Percy Cross'. The original, following initiatives from the Village Trust, was returned to Corbridge in 1975 and now stands, along with its plaque, by the door to the Vicar's Pele.

The opening of the annual Stagshaw Bank Fair was proclaimed from the steps of the cross. This fair was held each summer on Stagshaw Common some two miles north of Corbridge (beside what was Dere Street and is now the A68). The fair, with its likely origin in Saxon times, was certainly in existence in 1204 and not finally abandoned until 1930. During the Middle Ages the principal commodity sold seems to have been ironwork, for which Corbridge was well known, but later it was a market for livestock, especially sheep. Drovers from much of Scotland and northern England converged here twice a year, originally only at midsummer but later also at Whitsuntide, *'where, in three days, over 100,000 cattle, sheep, horses and swine changed hands'* – making it, at the time, the largest one-day fair in the country. The famous painting *'Proclaiming the Stagshaw Fair'* by Ralph Hedley (1882) hangs in the Laing Art Gallery in Newcastle. A print in St Andrew's Church identifies the figures.

Next to the Percy Cross is the **Market Place Pant** **5** which, in 1815, replaced an earlier drinking fountain (page 14). It has a plaque with the words *'ERECTED BY HUGH PERCY DUKE OF NORTHUMBERLAND ANNO MDCCCXV'*. On one side is a cow-tail handle implying that, initially, the water had to be pumped up. However, photos from later in the 19th century show water pouring from a faucet into a trough, suggesting that the 1836 pipeline from the spring in Carr's Field eliminated the need for pumping (page 14).

THE KING'S OVEN

THIS IS THE PAVEMENT OF THE COMMUNAL OVEN FOR THE BAKING OF THE VILLAGERS' BREAD AND MEAT. IT WAS FIRST RECORDED IN 1310 AS THE KING'S OVEN IN THE THEN ROYAL BOROUGH OF CORBRIDGE, AND WAS LAST IN USE IN THE 19TH CENTURY.

The upper storeys of the houses around the Market Place indicate that the terraces must have always been pleasant houses and probably date from the 1700s.

Number 9 appears to have two front doors but this is one of several examples in the village with a legacy of former years when one of the doors would have been used to gain access to a yard at the back – for collecting middens 200 years ago, for delivering coal 100 years ago and for storing wheelie bins today.

In the south-east corner is the Forum bookshop and above it an Indian restaurant. On the east is a florist (Watsonia), a café, a greengrocer (Stobo), an off-licence (Threshers) and a bakery (Nichols).

The building that now includes the bank was built in 1882 by the butcher Henry Ritchie. In 1920 the then tenant butcher, Donald Hall, sold the shop to **Barclays Bank** **6** and moved to Hill Street (page 33). On the south wall of the bank a plaque records that *'This land with access to the river was given to Corbridge by Barclays Bank Limited to mark the Silver Jubilee of H.M. Queen Elizabeth II in 1977'.*

Known as Barclays Garden, it was given a face-lift in 1996.

The building next to the bank, with the date 1835, has been unused for several years. Next to it used to stand the Old Bluebell Inn. When it was pulled down in 1890 an old lime-burning pit was discovered at a depth of 8 feet. It is possible that the pit was linked to the tanning industry. The inn was replaced initially by the Tynedale Hotel and later by an art café (now just a café) and an osteopathic clinic.

The King's Oven **7** was located near the west end of the church. Its exact position can still be seen by the square stones in the pavement found in front of the churchyard wall. First used in 1310 it was *'the communal oven for the baking of the villagers' bread and meat'.* It was last used, according to a plaque, in the 19th century.

Riverhill **8**, on the corner with Well Bank, was where the Red Cross met before moving to St Helen's Street in 1951. Built by Mr Lowery, a surgeon with a memorial in the churchyard, it is now a residential care home.

The old Market Cross.

On the 14th century map, the road leading north from the Market Place to present-day Hill Street was known as Market Gate, while the section beyond Hill Street was called Westgate (page 9). Even then both sides were totally built up. By the 1841 census and on the 1863 OS map, the whole was known as Watling Street.

West side

The first house after Well Bank (number 14) dates back to the early 1700s. It, like the adjacent properties, has walls of local block sandstone and a roof of blue slate. Number 15 has an ornate portico over the front door.

York House **9** (number 18), until recently Shu Shan, was built with light grey brick and has stone lintels and sills. The original plaque, now at first floor window level, has inscribed *'J D C Shu Shan 1876'*. This seems likely to be an anglicised version of the Chinese *'Xiao Shan'* (a common form of diminutive Chinese) meaning 'Little Hill'. While this could be a reference to a place in China, it could also be an old China hand's sense of humour referring to his house being either on top of a steep river cliff or on top of a steep garden!

Below: Watling Street c.1920.

Gresham House **10**, with its date of 1884, is a three-storey double-fronted house with twin gables and a roof with an extremely steep pitch (photo D, page 11). Like York House it is brick built and has stone quoins, sills and lintels. It housed the CIU social club until the club moved to new premises just off St Helen's Street. At present it is divided into an antiques shop, a local produce café and a contemporary glass and crafts centre.

The last property in this row (number 20) has, above the door lintel, a weathered plaque inscribed *'R L(?) 1855'*.

Dunkirk Terrace **11** was named *'Dunkirk'* on the 1863 OS map. It probably took its name from 'dun kirk', meaning 'grey-brown church', which Forster believed was the old Presbyterian place of worship. It is a short terrace, set back from Watling Street, of Victorian houses. In his book of 1974, Walter Iley called it *'Professors Row'* on account of three of the four houses being occupied by professors at what was then King's College in Newcastle upon Tyne. Number 1, **Watling House**, at the southern end of the terrace, has a Roman milestone in front of the wall of the house. It has the inscription *'CONSTANT IMP EBOR CXL MILIA LEG XX'*, which roughly translated means 'Emperor Constantine: Eboracum 140 miles: 20th Legion', followed by a depiction of a boar. (Eboracum was the Roman name for York and is where Constantine actually was when he was proclaimed Emperor on 25th July AD 306). Yet the milestone, despite its realistically weathered appearance, is a 'spoof' being carved c.1998 for a former lady owner of the house after she had won a relatively small sum of money in a competition. The milestone represents her winnings!

The most northerly property is **Sele House 12**. It was on this site in 1767 that a workhouse for the poor of the village was built, with Eliezer Birch Esquire of Cross House (page 30) being the chief instigator. The tender price was 109 pounds 17 shillings and 5 pence. According to old financial accounts, Birch donated £32 to *'ensure that it was soundly built with a slate as opposed to a thatch roof'*. The plot is identified on the 1780 tithe map as the *'Poor of Corbridge'* and is shown as a square building with a central courtyard. Dixon described the two-storey building as having *'stairs outside, at each end, leading to rooms upstairs'*. According to a Parliamentary Report in 1777, it housed up to 100 'paupers' who were lodged there at the expense of the parish of Corbridge. Each inmate was provided with food, clothing and bedding and was given 16 pence per week. In return they were expected to work at whatever they were best suited. The workhouse was closed and dismantled after the Hexham poorhouse opened in 1836.

The Wheatsheaf Inn **13**

The Wheatsheaf, set at the northern end of Watling Street, forms an attractive visual closure but one that creates two dangerous bends in the present-day road. The original building was a late 17th century farmhouse with several outhouses. Over a lintel in the old stable-yard to the east, is the date 1695 and the letters *'JL'* and *'RL'* (John Lumley and his father Ralph). On the 1780 tithe map, the owner of the land was given as Mary Lumley. It was listed as being an Inn in an 1827 trades directory (page 15).

Early photos show the building to have had two storeys with a third added about 1900. The area behind the Inn, now the car park, appears to have been used as a kitchen garden as an aerial photo (in the old Corbridge Health Centre) shows strips of land laid out for vegetables. The two crude heads in the yard, which may have represented Joy and Sorrow, are medieval and may have come from one of the three Corbridge churches destroyed in 1296. In recent years they have weathered so rapidly that their features are now unrecognisable. The statuette built into the outbuildings appears to have no archaeological significance.

East side

Numbers 2 to 6 were built using local block sandstone and blue slate. However, number 2 must have been built later as the plaque above its door says *'JR 1847'* in contrast with those above numbers 5 and 6 which have *'T.J.A. 1836'* and *'S.G.E. 1836'* respectively. Number 6 has two front doors separated by a former shop window. A photo taken about 1920 shows the shop belonging to Surtees Forster, a *'painter, glazier and paperhanger'*.

Warwick House **14** (number 7) was known as 'Oddfellows Hall' until it was converted about 1980. The hall comprised the full length of the first floor of the building. From the outside it now looks like

Above:
The Wheatsheaf corner.

two houses combined, with one of the earlier front doors blocked up. It has rubble stonework walls and sandstone quoins for doors and windows.

Numbers 8 to 11 are slightly taller than the previous buildings. Number 8 is double fronted and numbers 9 to 11 have, outside their front door, a cast-iron boot scraper and a stone threshold step. Number 11, on the corner with Hill Street, is a very popular café which, a century ago, was Edward Robson's *'Tailors, drapers and men's mercers'* and later Jean Hickleton's *'Menswear and baby clothes shop'* (page 35).

Below: The visual closure of Watling Street from the church tower.

WELL BANK and CARELGATE

The **Well Bank** runs west down to Well Green and the River Tyne. It was originally known as Corwell Chare (page 9), derived from the Cor-Well or Col-Well, which was located halfway down the bank (opposite number 1 St Andrew's Terrace). This well was later to be called St Andrew's Well and was, for several centuries during the medieval period, one of the two main sources of Corbridge's water supply (page 14). All visible trace was lost in 1992 when the area was inexplicably filled in. Just beyond the present-day car park was the Boating Green where, between the wars, the Amateur Rowing and Swimming Club had a boathouse, several rowing boats, a diving board and a putting green.

The Roman Stanegate, later known as **Carelgate** (Carlisle-gate), ran from Newcastle through the heart of today's village site, down Well Bank, along the north bank of the river to the crossing at Hexham (some 500 yards west of today's crossing) and westwards eventually to Carlisle. This road, though probably never more than a cart track that was frequently impassable, was the main and only route to the west until the turnpike was built.

Below: Well Green in the early 1920s.

Half a mile along this track was a water-powered corn mill of Anglo-Saxon origin and now converted for residential use. Just beyond it is the confluence of the Cor Burn, from which Corbridge derives its name, and the Tyne. It was here that Dere Street (or Watling Street), the old north–south Roman road, crossed the main river and intersected with Stanegate. The skirmish between Scots and Royalists in 1644 during the Civil War took place about here.

Diversion to Orchard Vale

A walk from Well Green takes you northwards behind Watling Street and Dunkirk Terrace to Orchard Vale. Orchard Vale 15, built in 1730 and formerly known as 'Geordie's Hole', is a three-storey Georgian house with a frontage facing the river that is largely unchanged. Above the entrance is the inscription '17.. JMK' – presumably 1731 and for John Morpeth and his wife Katherine. There is a Roman altar built into the north wall to the left of the door but its inscription is badly weathered. From here the path forks. The path to the east leads to the main road opposite the Wheatsheaf Inn while the path to the north continues to Town Barns, Trinity Terrace and the Roman site of Corstopitum.

Boating Green & Village, Corbridge.

STAGSHAW ROAD

This is the northern extension of Watling Street.

West side

St Mary's Church, along with Holy Trinity and St Helen's, was built in the early 13th century and, like the other two, was destroyed by the Scots in 1296 – the last stones were removed in 1770. The site was to the north of the lane that leads from the pant opposite the Wheatsheaf Inn down to Orchard Vale.

Bank Top was, from 1900 to 1918, the District Nurses' Hospital and was rented from the Beaufront Estate. It treated people who could not be adequately nursed in their own homes. It had two wards, one for men and one for women, each with two beds, together with two further rooms. An outbuilding, still standing, acted as the mortuary. It is now a private house with a garage that includes the date 1871 and a former church window.

Diversion to the west. Trinity Terrace consists of fourteen late 19th century houses. At the western end was the site of Holy Trinity Church and its graveyard, skeletons from which were uncovered when the foundations for the terrace were dug and later when various extensions were added. The footpath opposite the terrace leads to **Town Barns** 🔟 (where Catherine Cookson, the best-selling author, lived during the 1970s) and to the river at Well Green. Trinity Terrace itself continues to Corchester Towers, the Roman site of Corstopitum, Beaufront with its castle (built on the site of a mansion between 1836 and 1841) and Hexham.

Diversion to the north. The road leads northwards going under the A69 by-pass and up Stagshaw Bank (the former Roman Dere Street and now the A68) to Jedburgh and Edinburgh.

East side

Prior Manor was the site of the old Priory of Corbridge and was once owned by the Dean and Chapter of Carlisle Cathedral. The two present private houses are mainly 18th century and later but internal features are thought to include a 17th century fireplace. Just beyond, set in the street wall, is another of Corbridge's pants (page 14).

At the junction of St Helen's Lane, which some locals still call Sintlin's (or Synclen) Lane, and Stagshaw Road is **Charlotte Straker House** 🔟 . Before the First World War, when it was obvious that Bank Top was too small for the hospital needs of the growing village, a charitable fund was set up to obtain a larger property. In 1918, Joseph Straker bought Prior House, conveyed it to the trustees of the fund with an endowment of £5,000 and renamed it after his late wife. It was enlarged in 1930 and, after the creation of the NHS, it became part of the Northumbria Health Authority. When its future was in doubt in 1975, it

Left: Charlotte Straker House.

was transferred to the independent Charlotte Straker Project Trust. Numerous appeals and public collections have seen further extensions and improvements. Cookson Close, opened in 1992 in the grounds of Charlotte Straker House, consists of eight one- or two-person bungalows for elderly people.

Just south of here was the location of Foul Sike, a ditch that marked the northern boundary of Corbridge in medieval times (see Gormire, page 30).

West Cheynes, built in 1955 was, in the 1970s, the home of Ruth Ainsley, the author of children's books.

Below: Trinity Terrace c.1900 (top) and as it is today (bottom).

Trinity Terrace, Corbridge on Tyne.

This was originally called St Helen's Lane (page 9) and later Back Row. The 1780 tithe map shows only two or three buildings on each side of the street and at either end. The exception was a smithy situated halfway along the south side where Coopers Court now stands. At the 1841 census 62 people were living in this street, many being children. Of 17 residents in work there were 7 agricultural labourers, 3 labourers, 2 potters, 2 masons and 1 woodman, baker and miner.

Above: Causey House with its thatched roof in 1886.

The first two houses are numbered 1 (Watling Street) and 35. A house standing here in Tudor times was known as Cawsey Head and later as Causway Head. In 1594 it was sold to William Hudspeth and three sales later to Ralph Lumley whose initials appear with those of his son above the front door of the Wheatsheaf Inn (page 23), which is the adjacent building. In a photo of 1886 it is called Causey House and its thatched roof was believed to be the last one to remain in the village. These, and the houses opposite, are over 230 years old. Two un-numbered doors, one beside number 54 and the other between 48 and 50, were constructed to give access to yards behind the houses.

Red Arch is an old entrance to West End Terrace, a yard with modern in-fill (one house has the date 1998), and West Terrace. The name is believed to derive from the dust raised by Middlemiss's carts as they transported bricks from his works in West End Terrace (his bricks were red in colour in contrast to the yellow bricks of Jameson's – page 17).

Number 27 has a plaque, provided by the Village Trust, which states *'This house, built in 1820, became the first Methodist preaching house in Corbridge'*. It remained in use until 1865 when the present chapel in Princes Street was built.

The Red Cross moved into their Hall in 1951. When digging foundations for the re-development of the site in 2006, medieval floor tiles were discovered. By 2008 it will have become private housing.

Little Eden, on the south side, is a 1950s bungalow beside which is an alley. This leads to Orchard View which older residents refer to as 'The Mystery' as it led to a property with multi-occupancy so that nobody really knew who lived there. Indeed a cottage on the north side of Hill Street still has this name.

The two cottages are known as **The Duke's Cottages** ⑱ which their owner, the Duke of Northumberland, rented out cheaply. An attempt in 2006 to get English Heritage to have the buildings listed was refused but it was noted that *'they form an interesting part of the local street scene'*. They were refurbished in 2007.

The two houses next to the Duke's Cottages were Police Houses.

Opposite the Police Houses was a smithy, still marked on the 1920 OS map. Later, Bantham's spring factory occupied part of the site that is now a modern development with, under the entrance archway leading to **Coopers Court** and on the left, a large stone with the engraving *'WCP 1895'*. Next to it is the telephone exchange which some claim was the first in Britain to become automatic.

The lane next to the Police Houses leads to The Chains. The Chains initially were allotments set aside in 1849 by the Duke of Northumberland for the *'sustenance and recreation of Corbridgians'*. It acquired its name because each plot measured one chain, i.e. 22 yards, in length. A note, still attached to the rent book for the allotments, says *'1849. This year the allotments, seventy-four in number, on the*

Right: Red Arch and the first Methodist Preaching House.

north side of the village in a field called Hall Walls was granted by Algernon, Duke of Northumberland, to the villagers for spade cultivation at a moderate charge'. Hall Walls was, in the 13th to 15th centuries, the then manor house of the lords of Corbridge (it had decayed completely by 1663). The site became a holding area for prisoners-of-war during the Second World War and it is now the Chains Housing Development.

Located along this lane was St Helen's Church, built in the 12th century and destroyed by the Scots in 1296. In the early 19th century boys were still playing handball against the remnant chancel walls and climbing through its windows to reach pigeons' nests. By the end of that century all traces had gone and the site is now also part of the Chains Housing Development.

The **Parish Hall** 19 was, according to a plaque inside *'Erected by Edith Helen Straker-Smith in memory of her father Joseph Henry Straker'* in 1922. The hall was given to the *'Vicar and Council of the Parish Church'*.

The four houses opposite the Parish Hall, numbered 1 to 4 St Helen's Place, were built by Davison the builder on land bought from William Fairless in 1880. Number 2 was later bought in 1930 by William Tratham who had been Corbridge's first postman, in 1947 by George Twist the last shoemaker (page 17) and in 1988 by Bob Douglas, the author.

After the Second World War, Norwood Garage used to stand behind the present-day veterinary practice in Norwood House.

The lane next to it, now a car park for the Social Club, contained the Drill Hall where soldiers were garrisoned throughout the Second World War and which became a Youth Club until the 1960s.

On the south side, number 10, with its narrow front door, and numbers 12, 14 and 16 were built as flats, with two of the properties upstairs and two down. They form part of a block of Edwardian houses built in the first decade of the 20th century.

The small parade of shops were once a butcher's with its slaughter yard behind; a grocer's (both were part of the West Wylam and Prudhoe Co-op) also with a warehouse behind; and a draper's. Above them was the butcher's house, a reading room and a billiard room. The reading room was used as a canteen for the garrisoned soldiers during the war and was run by volunteers. The central part is now an Italian restaurant.

The four remaining houses on the south side (2a to 6) are over 200 years old. They are now owned by Milecastle Housing (see numbers 9 and 11 Princes Street). Number 8 was the Police Station before the present one was built in Aydon Road.

Above: The Parish Hall.

Below left:
The Duke's Cottages.

Below right: William Tratham, Corbridge's first postman, delivering letters c.1920.

The Town Hall building ⑳

Princes Street, named Prince Street on the 1780 tithe map and in the 1841 census, is dominated by the Town Hall building of 1887, built to commemorate the Golden Jubilee of Queen Victoria's accession. It is another example, like the Wheatsheaf and Monks Holme, of a visual closure at the end of a street that contributes to the overall attraction of the village. The building was designed, following an open competition, by Frank Emley. Frank, whose father was a prosperous mason, was sent to school in Switzerland before joining Oliver and Leeson who were then a leading firm of architects in the North-east. The building, typical of the late Victorian period, is described by Pevsner as *'a pretty Norman-Shavian stone building with four oriels and a central tower. The ornament is flowery acanthus'*. The foundation stone was laid by Mrs F.M. Laing of Farnley Grange whose husband had negotiated the purchase of the land and who donated the tower and the decorative sculptures. Above the figure holding up the crown is the famous Corbridge Seal (page 29). The oriel windows are supported by large corbels, while above the doorways are voussoir stones (page 13).

In 1901 the *Hexham Courant* reported that *'some good fairy had been transforming the inside of the Town Hall – and right well it had been done'*. Columns with ornamental capitals supporting semi-elliptical arches formed a dark background to the stage and fine scrollwork characterised the upper facades. It proved a popular venue for village activities such as dances, bazaars, lectures and concerts until the Parish Hall was opened in 1922. In 1941 the Hexham Entertainment Company, which owned the Forum and Queens Hall cinemas in Hexham, became the majority shareholder in the Town Hall Company and converted the hall into a cinema, and so it remained until 1958. Photos of the Town Hall building have always shown shops along the side facing Hill Street. Martin's Bank had premises here from 1895 until it was taken over by Barclays Bank in 1969 and closed. The Henderson Pharmacy has long been established (it belonged to J Sayburn Wilson in the mid-1930s) while John Graham relocated the Post Office and his newsagent shop here from Hill Street in 1997.

The Town Hall building with architectural detail (below).

Left: Coigns Corner.

Above: The ancient seal of Corbridge.

South from the Town Hall building

Prior to the 19th century, this part of Princes Street was wider than it is today. One reason why it became narrower was the building of the Methodist Chapel at the junction with Hill Street (page 33).

An extremely narrow footpath leads past the public toilets (which may need a visit even if of no historic or architectural interest) to the **Coigns** ㉑ (until the early 20th century, the Coins). The name is derived from a word meaning 'corner' and therefore it is tautology when local people refer to this, a meeting place for centuries, as 'Coigns Corner'. In the mid-18th century a waggoner called Johnson, who made twice-weekly journeys between Hexham and Newcastle, used to stop here to impart 'the news' to an eagerly awaiting audience. Some fifty years later, about 1800, one newspaper a week was delivered to Mr Winship, the owner of the Angel Inn, and read aloud. An equally important function of this location dating from the early 19th century was the hiring of reapers at harvest time. Men, their children and sometimes even their wives, gathered at 7.00 a.m. hoping to get work for the day. Those selected, often as many as 150, were then transported by long carts to surrounding farms.

The building opposite the west gable end of the Angel Inn was a branch of Walter Willson's until it was demolished in 1970 for a road-widening scheme that was subsequently abandoned. The resultant open space was later converted as a millennium project by the Parish Council (which now owns it) and the Village Trust. It has seats, an information board describing places in the village and, set into the wall, a replica of one of the ancient seals when Corbridge was a borough (13th century). The original seal of 1235 (some books say 1233) had a cross separating four men's heads in profile, each wearing a headpiece with a nasal defence. It has been suggested that the cross is not a religious symbol but represents four soldiers defending the point where Dere Street is crossed by Stanegate (page 4).

Below: 'The Hirings' of reapers in the 1880s.

PRINCES STREET

North from the Town Hall building – west side

This part of Princes Street has been known as Gormire Row (1863 OS map) and Gormire (1924 OS map). The name Gormire seems to be derived not from a street but from the medieval ditch that surrounded Corbridge in the east. This is referred to in deeds of 1591 as *'the common water-gate called Gormire'* (compare Foul Sike page 25).

The first buildings, which include the side of the **Golden Lion** ㉒ (page 33) and numbers 5 and 7, are imposing. Built in the mid-18th century, they are three storeys high and consist of block sandstone which, according to the plaque in front of the Golden Lion (but which contains inaccuracies), came from Dilston Hall. Number 7 still has the window from when it was Norman Robson's butcher's shop

and two impressive hooks from which carcasses were hung. The shop closed in the late 1970s. It is believed that this building was used as a barracks when dragoons were stationed in Corbridge in the 18th century and it is possible that General Wade stayed here whilst constructing the Military Road in the 1750s.

Numbers 9 and 11, together with the end houses in St Helen's Street (page 27), form a terrace of early 18th century stone cottages. Some years ago they fell into disrepair and, rather than modernise them, the owner surrendered them to Hexham RDC which later became part of Tynedale Council and which in turn sold them to Milecastle Housing. They have been modernised at considerable expense but without, fortunately, detracting from their external appearance.

Across St Helen's Street is **Cross House** ㉓, built about 1756 by Eliezer Birch who is remembered as a church warden and for his philanthropic works (Iley spells his name Eleizer). These included donating one half of the costs for the original clock for St Andrew's Church, erecting the first village pant (located further up Princes Street and which still issues water – page 14) and encouraging the building of the workhouse for the poor on Watling Street (page 22). Yet Birch was a mysterious figure. In 1991, R.J. Malden, son of an earlier vicar of Corbridge, revealed him to be a wealthy young man who in 1745 acted as a government spy during the Jacobite uprising, made a dramatic escape from the rebels and retired to Corbridge on grounds of ill-health. He acquired considerable land in Corbridge and came to live here for 17 years before his death in 1767. He is buried in the churchyard.

Cross House, reputedly built using stone from the ruins of nearby Dilston Hall, is an enigma. It has one entrance but two front doors – one being slightly different from the other. Despite having the appearance of two houses, there is evidence of earlier internal interconnecting doors. The rear garden is similarly divided into two by a brick wall, with the whole of the property surrounded by a high stone wall. A more likely, but less interesting, reason is that Birch himself occupied half the house while the other half, that to the east, was for his servants. A more interesting, but unsubstantiated, reason is that he built the house this way so that his mistress and her family could live in one half, and he in the other. Access to the stables to the rear was through an imposing gateway to the west side of the house. Walter Iley was living here when he wrote his *Corbridge – Border Village* in the 1970s.

Below: Cross House.

Next to Cross House was, in 1827, the Golden Fleece Inn and later, according to the trades directory of 1886, the Beerhouse. The Inn was believed to have opened at 6.00 a.m. to serve workers on their way to Jameson's (page 17). It is said many succumbed to alcohol and missed work! By 1904 it belonged to F.M. Laing, a wine and spirit merchant who had earlier negotiated the purchase of land for the Town Hall building (page 28). It is now a private residence.

A narrow building called **Eastgate** ㉔, now part of a terrace, was originally a tollhouse created when the Aydon turnpike road was built to connect with the new Military Road in the 1750s.

The original **vicarage** ㉕ on Aydon Road, shown on the 1780 tithe map, was an L-shaped building. It was through the pleading of an 18th century vicar, the Rev. John Walton, that Corbridge was included in the Enclosures Act of 1776. In 1829 when Henry Gipps was appointed vicar he requested a survey of the property. It was confirmed to be in such a poor state of repair that it was demolished in 1831 and a new one built on the present site. This was enlarged in 1887 when a new vicar, the Rev. Francis Richardson, arrived with his wife, seven children and three maids. During the installation of central heating by the Rev. R.C. Malden in 1960, a lead-lined coffin-shaped bath, with two taps but no outlet, was uncovered under the floorboards. The vicarage, when sold in 1984, was divided into the two houses of today. Its former coach house still remains a private residence.

Two old, semi-detached cottages near St Helen's Lane are similar in style to the Duke's Cottages on St Helen's Street (page 26).

Diversions to the north

Beyond St Helen's Lane and Corbridge First School are two lanes.

Milkwell Lane leads north-west and passes the former Walkers Pottery (page 17) with, according to Pevsner, *'its two impressive early 19th century "bottle ovens" and pair of Newcastle "horizontal kilns" which makes it unique in the north of England'*. In the early 1970s the Village Trust was seriously concerned about the structural stability of the kilns and after lengthy negotiations the Industrial Monument Trust (now the Tyne and Wear Building Preservation Trust) agreed with the owners to guarantee the preservation of the kilns for 99 years. The Village Trust is still monitoring the site.

Deadridge Lane (referred to as Dithridge Lane in a 1930s village guide) leads, via a footpath, to the A69 by-pass and Aydon. It was the location of the former Corbridge nine-hole golf course.

Aydon Road leads to Aydon, Halton, the Military Road, Hadrian's Wall and Matfen Hall. Aydon Castle is a fortified manor house restored by English Heritage which, in summer, is open to the public. Halton Church, Saxon in origin, is also open to the public, unlike Halton Castle which is the private residence of the Blackett family. The Military Road was built after the Jacobite uprising of 1745 when General Wade and his army frequently became bogged down passing along old Carelgate (page 24) en route to confronting the rebels in Carlisle. This new road, which was a turnpike two miles to the north, was built between 1751 and 1755.

North from the Town Hall building – east side

Returning down Princes Street

The **Wesleyan Methodist Chapel** ㉖, in Gothic style, replaced in 1865 the earlier chapel in St Helen's Street (page 26). It cost £1,600 and could seat 360 people. It was restored in 1895 at a cost of £400 when the seating was extended and a new 'heating apparatus' was installed.

The pant, south of Appletree Lane, was the one donated by Eliezer Birch (page 14). It still provides a reliable flow although the quantity varies with the seasons. Appletree Lane was called Emms Lane on the 1780 tithe map and School Lane after a Church of England school was built here in 1855 on land belonging to the Greenwich Hospital Estates. Due to 'unsanitary conditions' and the absence of a playground, the school was completely rebuilt in 1908; it closed in 1970. At one time the school housed the Joseph Viney Museum.

Orchard House ㉗, aptly named and with a plaque giving its date as 1887, is a substantial brick building that is somewhat out of character with the surrounding stone houses. During the 1930s it was advertised as *'Misses Gallon, Apartments, Attendance'*. The Gallons also ran fish and chip shops in both Watling Street and Front Street, a baker's in Front Street and owned the orchard in Orchard Crescent. For much of the 18th and 19th centuries the area bounded by Princes Street and Main Street was entirely taken up by extensive orchards, as reflected by the names 'Appletree Lane' and the secluded 'Orchard Crescent' (behind the dentist's).

Above: One of the meat hooks from outside the former butcher's shop at number 7 Princes Street (below)

Hill Street, extending between Watling Street and Princes Street, was given its name in 1897 at the first meeting of the newly created Parish Council. Before that, the western part (behind St Andrew's Church) had been known as Scramble Gate (and before that Fishshamble Gate, Fishmarket Gate and Horsemarket Street) and the eastern section as Heron's Hill (page 9). The name Scramble Gate may have been derived from the old custom of 'scrambling' for money thrown by newly married couples as they left the church. By c.1500 the whole street, and all the land three-quarters of a mile to the north, was owned by Roger Heron who was a kinsman of Sir Cuthbert Heron of Chipchase Castle. In 1714 the land passed to Nicholas Greenwell and in 1738 it was bought by John Aynsley, a Hexham lawyer. It remained in his family for the next 100 years before passing to the Errington family, who also owned Beaufront Castle one mile west of Corbridge. The 1780 tithe map shows buildings along the entire north side of the street. Today the street is divided into two by a ridge, with the area to the east forming a small commercial core.

Below: Western end of Hill Street c.1900 (top) and as it is today (bottom).

The doorway of Heron House.

Heron House 28.

In 1830, Sir Roger Errington sold Heron House, which stands near the highest point and in a central position in the street, to a tailor called Aitken. He put a new front on the house and had his own and his wife's initials carved as a marriage mark above the door: *ARL*. The next owner was a joiner and local coffin maker called Fairless. A 1920 photo shows the building to be a confectioner's shop run by Mrs Forster with, on the outside, an advert for *'Stagshaw Bank coals'* delivered by her husband Tommy who ran a haulage firm. Since 1960 it has been a coffee house, an art gallery, an antiques outlet and now a widely-known delicatessen. Pevsner dates the property, with its shouldered pediment doorway, decorated architrave and string course, to about 1700 (page 13).

West from Heron House

During most of the 20th century, and until 1997, the village Post Office was located in what is now an art gallery. There is still a post-box in the wall.

Saunders and Pughe's building with its mullion window, and number 30 with the date 1700 on its original lintel, are two of several surviving properties that are 300 years old.

The Blue Bell 29, formerly the New Blue Bell, is listed in a trades directory of 1827. The landlord, at one time, was the grandfather of George Hall the butcher.

Opposite, and within the churchyard, is **St Andrew's Cottage** 30. A building is shown here on the 1780 tithe map. This is the best vantage point from which to see the small eagle set low down and to the left on the church tower (page 18).

This end of the street may once have been part of the churchyard, as many burials have been discovered here during subsequent road-works.

East from Heron House

Numbers 16 (Orvis) and 14 are large properties each with its own distinctive design and architecture. The doorways, which are adjacent, have two large lintels resting on three large vertical stones. Above the lintels is a string course (page 13). Each house

Corbridge. Hill Street.

has an oriel window and, under their roofs and that of Heron House, are stone corbels (page 13).

Woodburn House ③① (number 12) was a private house until the optometrist moved here from the Market Place in 1974.

The present-day Co-op was previously a branch of Alldays and before that Walter Willson's, which moved here when their building on Coigns Corner was demolished (page 29). Before that it was a group of terraced cottages.

The Golden Lion ㉒ is a three-storey building constructed of sandstone blocks brought from Dilston Hall in 1768 at the time of its demolition (page 30).

On the opposite corner is the former **United Methodist Chapel** ㉜. The original chapel, built in 1864, was replaced in 1885 with the present-day building with its Gothic-style windows, copied from those in the old chapel (recently restored) at Dilston Hall, and door. The initials on some of the bricks denote sponsors. The congregation joined that of the Princes Street chapel in 1938 and the building was sold. The first floor is now the Public Library, which the County Council in 2007 seem set to close, and the ground floor is the Tourist Information Centre.

The butcher's shop holds deeds from the early 1700s. The Hall family, who at different times were landlords of the Angel Inn and the New Blue Bell Inn, moved here in the early 1920s from the Market Place (page 20). The Halls did their own slaughtering behind the shop and this continued until the mid-1990s, some five years after George Hall retired (the shop still retains the family name).

The five terraced cottages to the west of the butcher's are built on land that, on the 1780 tithe map, belonged to the Greenwich Hospital Estates. (The Commissioners of the hospital looked after, on behalf of the Crown, land that included most of Dilston. After the execution of the 3rd Earl of Derwentwater in 1716, the remainder of Dilston was confiscated.) The two properties to the east were built in the 1880s while the three to the west were converted in the 1930s from old farm buildings at a cost of £1,100.

The art shop and Penny Plain were only built in the early 1990s but easily fit into the building style of the street.

Above: The information board from the Golden Lion.

Left: The 'hill'.

Below: The north side of Hill Street looking west.

MIDDLE STREET

Middle Street, known as Synodgatsyde in 1330 and Sydgate in 1379, had its present name by 1702 (page 9). Although un-named on the 14th century town plan, it appears to have been lined with buildings even at that early date. The 1863 OS map shows that the properties were laid out in a similar way both to the rest of the village centre and to those of today. They were mainly rectangular with a small road frontage and, on the north side, room at the rear for gardens, orchards and vegetable patches that extended back to Hill Street. Since then in-fill has taken place with the additional buildings leaving little space for cultivation. Three alleyways leading off Middle Street, including Sydgate Mews, give access to the rear of the properties where it is possible to trace this development.

From the Market Place end it can be seen that the buildings on the south side are built to a regular curve whereas several of those on the north jut out from the general line causing the pavement to vary in width. Iley, writing in the early 1970s, called it *'a happy street'* and refers to the baker, newsagent, fashion shop, draper, inn and restaurant, ironmonger, fish shop, hairdresser and wool shop.

The first building on the north side consists of a yellow brick which was made in Corbridge and is a feature of the local clays. It was put up to commemorate the Diamond Jubilee of Queen Victoria – hence the plaque *'Jubilee Buildings 1897'*.

Numbers 21 to 27 opposite form a short terrace of typical early 18th century cottages. Robert Forster (see 26 Front Street) was living at number 25 when his book on Corbridge was published in 1881.

The display windows of most of the shops in Middle Street, with their wood-carved mullions and fascias, are virtually as they were in the 19th century. Likewise their internal construction shows many features of earlier times. **Sydgate House** ㉝ is double-fronted with ornate windows and doorway. Its present name of 'Acanthus' means *'a formalised leaf ornament with thick veins and frilled edge'*.

Right: The south side of Middle Street c.1900 and the same view as it is today.

The Black Bull **34**, originally a 17th century farmhouse, now consists of two joined mid-18th century buildings. That to the west is the older. It has, under the lintel of the original entrance door now partially blocked up to make a window for the present-day bar, the date 1755 and *'Marg US and EU'* for two Usher sisters. It was originally called Usher House after the family who built it and who lived here between 1755 and 1769. The Black Bull, though not listed as a public house in 1827, was extended to take in what was originally a private house to the east. This house, dated 1765, had two doorways, both of which still have their original pediments. The eastern doorway which, in a photo taken in 1950, had a sign above it saying *'bar'* (page 6), has also, since then, been partially blocked up and now forms a window for the restaurant. The adjacent alleyway used to lead to several cottages that were still lived in after the Second World War but which have since been incorporated into the Black Bull itself.

The eastern end of Middle Street has for over a hundred years been devoted to haute couture for the well-dressed woman. In the early 20th century there was *'Pearsons – tailor, draper, millinery and dressmaking'* before it became Jean Hickleton's *'Ladies outfitters'*. Jean also had a menswear and baby clothes shop where the Watling Street café now stands and a wool shop at 17 Front Street. In 1970 Norma James **35** moved into the Middle Street premises where she achieved a national reputation. Sadly for Corbridge, she decided in 2007 to retire.

Eastwards from Norma James's used to be, in order, Dixon's the newsagent, Ellis's Boutique, Chaffey's the baker (known for its meat pies; it is now Savages the solicitors) and, where there is now public open space, Walter Willson's (page 29).

Number 7 opposite has the date 1859.

At the eastern end, opposite Coigns Corner and at the main crossroads of the village, is **Lloyds Bank TSB 36**. The three-storey Edwardian building, with imitation voussoirs and slightly bevelled pediments above the two doors (page 13), was built in 1909 on a dominating site overlooking the bridge. It is said that the plans for the bank were mixed up and that this building was meant for either Bishop Auckland or Cambridge.

Far left: The decorative shop window and doorway of Sydgate House.

Above: The Black Bull.

Left: The north side of Middle Street looking west.

MAIN STREET

This has been the main road to Newcastle for several centuries. In earlier times it was known both as Eastgate and Thornburghgate but by the 14th century it was commonly referred to as Smithygate (page 9) as this was where Corbridge's significant medieval iron trade was carried on (the ironwork of the door of Vicar's Pele may have come from here). The 1780 tithe map and the 1863 OS map show a pattern of housing similar to that of today except that the gardens and orchards of the houses on the north side extended back to Princes Street whereas those to the south were even then running down to the river. Many of the large houses were built, or extended, by wealthy merchants, based in Newcastle, who came to reside in Corbridge after the coming of the railway.

The Angel Inn ㊲

The Angel Inn, a grade 1 listed building, is 10 bays wide and is the oldest inn in Corbridge. Inside the west porch is a 17th century arched doorway and above the sundial on the front facade is the date 1726 and the letters 'E W A' – for Edward and Anne Winship. To the east is a mullion window. In the centre of the 'Hotel and Restaurant' sign on the front wall is a Guild Mark for the Incorporated Company of (stone) Masons of Newcastle. Inside, on the hearth, is a painted model of a stone hunting dog. The original, which some believe (without much evidence) to have been Roman, can be seen on old photographs standing on the gable of the roof that faces the river. In the 18th century The Angel was known as 'The Head Inn' and was the stopping place for the Newcastle to Carlisle mail coach – the stables being in the present-day car park. Indeed, grooves worn in the stone window frames are believed to have been caused by chained mail-bags. Nineteenth century photos show three linked buildings, the central one being the oldest. At one time the landlord was the great-grandfather of George Hall the butcher. Until 1934 the western end, now the restaurant, was a cottage. The land on the opposite corner, now containing Bridge House and The Coign (page 41), used to be the Angel Inn's allotment. In 2007, when owner John Gibson was having an extension for a new restaurant added, the old wall flanking Princes Street collapsed showing, probably like many other old buildings in the village, an absence of foundations. It did, however, expose two skeletons that were not, as first rumoured, debtors to the Angel, but in fact were dated to the 13th century medieval period. Archaeologists also found distinct burning areas, metal slag and a bronze cauldron handle, suggesting that this was a site for medieval bronze and iron workings. If so it will be one of only 30 such medieval workings in the country (there are two others in the county). Fire evidence of this period could also fit with the sacking of the village by the Scots in 1296 (page 5).

Above: The Angel Inn c.1890 and as it is today (right).

North side

Stonecroft 38 has been owned by the Bishop family since around 1930. Until 1987, when they were demolished, a pair of cottages stood in front of the property. The west cottage was lived in by local plumber Archie Moffett whose workshop was up the lane to the rear in what is now an antiques shop. From the east cottage the Rewcastle family ran an ice-cream and coffee shop from before the war until 1955.

Bishops Garage 39. J. Bishop & Son started trading in Main Street from two workshops, the first bought from W. Turnbull the painter and glazier in 1920, the second from Fairless the joiner in 1937. Jack Bishop, a Welsh man and motor mechanic, came to Corbridge after being chauffeur to Captain Cuthbert of Beaufront Castle. From 1920 to 1928 cars were refuelled from funnel and jerry cans which were filled from a large tank at the rear of the premises. Hand-operated pumps were introduced in 1928. The family, who initially lived in Main House, built Eastcote in 1938. During the Second World War, car parts were manufactured in the rear tool shop. The family started selling cars in 1934 and expanded into Hexham in 1956 when Bishops Garages Ltd was formed. In 1983, the front of Main House was demolished to make room for the present forecourt. As the business grew in Hexham, the Corbridge site was adapted for fuel, servicing and body repairs. In 1999, the Corbridge garage became a petrol station and convenience store and in 2006 new pumps were installed. It has remained a family firm, Julian being the great-grandson of the founder.

Dunedin 40 is an imposing double-fronted house built in 1876 (the date is on the gable) by Dr McLean, a wealthy Edinburgh doctor. When he bought it from the Walker family it was part of Old Barns Farm. The front door and an upstairs window have fine swan-neck pediments (page 13). The consulting rooms, now a flat, remained until the whole property was bought from Dr Turnbull by John Bishop, son of Jack, in 1956.

Eastfield Cottages 41 are a pair of early 19th century cottages – Holly Cottage to the west and Eastfield to the east. Eastfield, with the initials and date of *'B L 1814'* (Bartholomew Lumley of Eastfield House) on the lintel, was the home of the Walker family.

Eastfield House 42, which appears to be two houses joined together, was at one time lived in by Bartholomew Lumley, a surgeon from Northallerton who died in 1893. The property was bought by Charles Mackenzie who went on to own not only Eastfield House but also what is now Smiths Gore, the two Eastfield Cottages, Lumley Cottage, the three Orchard Cottages (at the northern end of the footpath behind the property) and Bishop's car

park. Mackenzie sold parts of this in the 1920s and the remainder, including Eastfield House, to the Corbridge Gas Company in 1936 for £1,200. The Gas Company in turn sold Lumley Cottage in 1941 (it is now a refurbished private house). The Northern Gas Board, so-named after nationalisation in 1949, sold Eastfield House to Smiths Gore & Company in 1964 for £9,000. The western part, with its upper mullioned windows and attic dormer, is one of the oldest houses in the village. It is now partly hidden by the shop front (erected by the Gas Company) of Smiths Gore, the land agents and chartered surveyors which was founded in London in 1845. Smith was one of the two original founders while Gore became the first ever winner of the men's singles championship at Wimbledon in 1877.

Above: Main Street looking east in the late 1940s. The boy is thought to be John Bishop.

Below: Dunedin House with architectural detail.

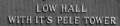

LOW HALL
WITH IT'S PELE TOWER

THE OLDEST HOUSE IN CORBRIDGE DATING IN PART FROM
THE 13TH CENTURY. THE DOORWAY OF THE CROSS-PASSAGE
ENTRY TO THE ORIGINAL HALL HOUSE IS VISIBLE BELOW
THE SOUTH WEST CORNER OF THE TOWER AND A SMALL
13TH CENTURY LANCET WINDOW CAN BE SEEN IN THE WEST
GABLE. THE EAST END OF THE HOUSE WAS HEIGHTENED
INTO A TOWER IN THE 15TH CENTURY. THE HOUSE WAS FURTHER
ALTERED IN THE 17TH CENTURY AND SUBSTANTIALLY EXTENDED
IN THE 1890'S.

Low Hall 43

Low Hall is believed to be the oldest residence in the village. Some parts of the original pele may be from 1195 but the core of the house consists of a 13th or 14th century rectangular block with a ground floor hall. The eastern end was raised in a three-storey pele tower by the Baxter family in the 15th century, hence 'Baxter's Tower' (the family was first mentioned in the village in 1381). The main block was remodelled in the 16th century and the large mullioned windows were added about 1675. There is a descriptive plaque on the front wall. The sundial on the house frontage, similar to the one on St Andrew's Church, has the date 1700. Mr Reginald Gibson bought the house in 1674 but was to lose it and his life (he died in prison) by backing, along with Lord Derwentwater of Dilston, the wrong side in the 1715 Jacobite uprising. Low Hall was then bought successively in 1716 by the same John Aynsley who owned Heron House (page 32); in 1881 by John Walker who did restoration work and added the extension to the rear in about 1890; and in 1895 by Harry Edwards of Byethorne. It was taken over by the North East Electric Board during the Second World War when part of a Roman tablet was found in the tower recording the erection, in AD 162, of a large building by the 20th Legion to two of their Emperors. Low Hall was bought in 1947 by Elliot Common of Common Bros Shipping Line (see Byethorne, page 40), and by the present owners in 1995. It has recently undergone an extensive programme of restoration.

Far right: The 13th century lancet window in Low Hall.

The Stables, to the north-east of Low Hall, was a brewery during the 19th century, although the only remaining evidence is a cellar in the small building nearest to the Pele Tower. The brewery was bought by Mr Edwards of Monks Holme in 1892 for his horses – all the new buildings that he had added were purpose-built as stables. The groom lived at number 1 Springfield Cottage. Army ambulances were stationed in the yard during the Second World War when Corbridge was a garrison town.

Diversion to the east

Main Street becomes the Newcastle Road and passes the new Health Centre, built in 2007, to Howden Dene (former home of the Straker family who were village benefactors), Thornbrough and the Styford roundabout where the A68 leads to the south (joining the Roman Dere Street) and the A69 to Newcastle.

Diversion to the south

This leads down Spoutwell Lane, earlier known as the 'Drift' or the 'Drove Road' named from the time when the only way for animals to cross the

river was by the ford at the foot of the lane. The enormous wall to the west has a height of 22 feet (nearly 7 metres) and was built in the late 19th century by Harry Edwards, the then owner of Byethorne. Further down the lane is the Spout Well that has never knowingly run dry (page 14) and the entrance to Springfield Haugh, a cedar bungalow built in 1947 for Miss Reed, formerly of Byethorne.

The ford itself was used either when the road bridge was in disrepair or by cattle-owners avoiding the payment of tolls. It was also used by Royalists when they surprised an army of Scots in 1644. It was in the river bank close to the ford that the famous Corbridge Lanx, a silver dish, was discovered by a young girl in 1734. Weighing 148 ounces (4,200 grams) and measuring 20 by 15 inches (50 by 38 cm), it is adorned with a group of mythological deities. Originally claimed by the Duke of Northumberland, it has since passed to the British Museum in lieu of death duties.

South side

The houses on this side have been extensively altered, especially since the advent of the railway in early Victorian times.

Monks Holme 44

Monks Holme is an imposing early 17th century Jacobean building. It dominates the eastern end of Main Street providing another example, along with the Wheatsheaf and Town Hall buildings, of a visual closure so typical of the village. It was listed in the trades directory of 1827 as the New Inn (page 15), one of eight public houses in the village and owned by the Gibson family. On the north side is a small window where ale was passed to horsemen to save them having to dismount (it is so low they must have been using Shetland ponies!) while underground is a cellar with a barrel-shaped ceiling. The house was bought in 1890 by Mr Edwards, a Newcastle dock owner and the then owner of Byethorne. It was he who, in 1891, heavily restored the frontage and added the porch with its pediment although the attic dormers are original, as are possibly some of the finials. The mounting block and two adjacent cottages have long since gone.

East Lodge used to be separated from Monks Holme by Little Lane, a track that no longer exists.

Above right: Byethorne in the late 1880s, with its three storeys and clock tower, and as it is today (above).

Byethorne ㊺

Byethorne (Byethorn on some earlier OS maps) is a large house, set in 25 acres of grandiose gardens, parkland and woodland.

1786 The house was built on land that was bought for £170 from Reginald Gibson of Brocksbushes. The house, then named 'The Willows', had a kitchen garden and a south-facing terrace which overlooked fields that led down to the river, the course of which was further north than it is today.

1867 Bought for £3,450 by Harry Edwards, a Tyneside shipbuilder. He re-named it 'Byethorne' after the second ship he built. He purchased further adjoining properties and extended and improved the house and its grounds. He built a third floor and an impressive clock tower over the entrance and added water gardens, tennis courts, a vinery and glasshouses that extended 200 feet along the high wall with Spoutwell Lane. The wall was built to hide two houses that Edwards had granted permission to be built in the lane. He also blocked the northern channel of the Tyne which, until then, had forked through the grounds creating an island. The former channel is marked by a line of trees and still floods when river levels are very high.

1898 Edwards died but the property remained in the family.

1920 Sold for £11,000 to Reed's, the brewing family. They removed the top storey and had the clock tower taken down, supposedly to save money. The stones were used to protect the river bank from erosion.

1928 Bought by the Common shipping family for £7,750 (see Low Hall). They moved their office here during the Second World War but did little to look after the grounds.

1971 The executors of Miss Common fragmented the estate, selling off various houses and parts of the gardens to four different owners.

1972 Purchased by the future Sir Lawrie Barratt, the national house builder. By 1984 he had bought back most of the land, the two lodges and the four estate houses previously owned by Harry Edwards. The grounds now contain numerous Italian marble and stone statues; ponds, fountains and cascades; soft fruit, vegetable, herb, rose and water gardens; an arboretum of over 200 trees; an aviary and peacock house; together with extensive areas of lawn and parkland. It also includes woodland on the south bank of the Tyne opposite the house.

1992 Arthur Wilson, the head gardener for 20 years, collected for the third time in five years the Northumberland in Bloom trophy for the best garden open to the public. (The garden is no longer open.)

Vine Cottage and Ivy Cottage **46**, shown on old OS maps to be on land once belonging to the Byethorne Estate, are both detached and double-fronted.

Newstead **47**, set down a short drive, was built in 1934 on land that previously had included farm buildings and a gin gang. It still contains a substantial Second World War air raid shelter built for Mr Towers, the then Managing Director of Redheads shipyard on the Tyne.

Corbridge House **48**, known as the White House in the late 18th century, was, according to Dixon (1912), one of the most important houses in the village. He claimed that it was the first property to have both a slate roof and a front garden, the latter taken from the wide street. The house is recorded as belonging to the Reed family as far back as 1838 and, apart from a short break between 1889 and 1915, remained in that family for over 130 years.

Laurel House and Havigal **49** were shown as one building on John Bell's map of 1778 and was only divided into two in 1875 after George Crake bought the house for £1,145. It is believed that the main stone south wall is part of the original building and was retained when the present frontage with its squared stones and dressed coigns was added in Victorian times.

Waverly House **50** is a random stone-fronted property built in 1849. Behind it **Lane End**, formerly Prospect House, is located at the end of a short, narrow, paved and cobbled lane. Lane End was built in 1878 as a 'Gentleman's Residence' by the then owner of Waverly House. Before 1849 this plot was a smithy's shop with stables. When Lane End was built it was connected to Waverly House by the 18th century stables to form one property which was then converted into ground-floor kitchens with three bedrooms above. Waverly House later became the village Post Office when it was moved here from Front Street in 1901 – inside there is still a hole in the wall where the post-box used to be. From 1948 to 1974 Lane End was owned by Leslie Bird of Bird's Laundry, with his chauffeur occupying Waverly House. In 1984 an upstairs corridor linked the two houses before the then owner 'sold a bedroom' to the owner of Waverly House for £5,000, thus creating a flying freehold.

Holly House and Glenthorne **51** are, from an architect's point of view, possibly the most aesthetically attractive houses in the village. Thought to be late 18th or early 19th century, although looking younger than the neighbouring Waverly House, they are double-fronted with dressed quoins and ashlar stones believed to have come from Dilston Hall (page 33). They must, however, be older than the Angel Radcliffe as the brick chimney extension was needed to cope with the higher, newer property.

The pant **52** was erected in 1818 by public subscription (page 14).

The Angel Radcliffe **53**, formerly Roman Lodge, the Radcliffe House Hotel and then Riverside House, was built in the late 1760s also using stone taken from Dilston Hall. The rear wing was added about 1919. The house was at one time a convalescent home with rather unattractive buildings in the grounds (which the 1924 OS map names as a 'surgery' and was demolished in 1991 to make way for the new dwelling of Radcliffe House). It was acquired by the Angel Inn in 2007.

Westfield and Westfield Cottage **54**. The deeds date back to 1687 when, until the Enclosures Act in 1776, the property possessed two butts in the East Field (near the Spout Well) which were passed on with each conveyance. Westfield was sold in 1729 for £42. Nicholas Stokoe, who died here in 1733, has the oldest gravestone in the churchyard (page 19). There is a rather worn stone head built into the garden wall of either Roman or medieval origin.

The Coign **55**, on the corner as its name suggests, was built in 1900 as a District Nurses' home for the benefit of the village by Miss Edwards of Byethorne (page 40) in memory of her father Harry. It was intended for the treatment of all patients (apart from those with infectious diseases) of the poorer classes although they were expected to pay a small weekly charge. Wealthier patients were also admitted but were expected to contribute to their support. The architects Armstrong and Wright of Newcastle designed it in an 'Arts and Crafts style' with echoes of the work of Voysey, on land formerly owned by Newcastle Breweries. By 1914, the building was considered to be too small for the community and sold. It was sold again in 1920 for £1,400.

Bridge House **56** was, in the mid-20th century, a doctor's surgery. It had a brass plate by its door inscribed *'Doctors Gass, Basham and Hird'*.

Above: The Main Street Pant.

Above: Bridge House.

Below: Holly House and Glenthorne.

FRONT STREET

Front Street was known in 1350 as Narrowgate and by 1778 as Water Row (page 9). The south side is built on the edge of a steep slope, or river cliff, above the Tyne. Here the rear of the houses face the street while their fronts take advantage of the view to the south which includes their own sunny gardens, the river and its bridge, Prospect Hill and Dilston. This street of brown-grey stone buildings curves sufficiently to be hidden from the busy Market Place. Although now a quiet, mainly residential one-way street, with arguably the most interesting of housing styles in the village, it had listed in an 1886 trades directory the following businesses: the Post and Telegraph Office (with four dispatches to, and two from, Newcastle on weekdays – a contrast to today's service!), draper, draper and tailor, grocer and provisioner, dressmaker, plumber, veterinary surgeon, watchmaker and the Boot and Shoe Public House.

Number 1 is where three generations of the family of Robert Forster (see number 26 below) had a blacksmith's forge.

Numbers 3 and 5, recently converted into one house and now known as **Riversbank** 57, has a metal plaque high above the front door to indicate that fire insurance was paid up to date and, therefore, that the fire brigade would attend if required. There has been a building of one sort or another on this site since the early 1400s.

Number 7 is a large pre-1790 double-fronted property. It was bought by the vet, Alexander Chivas, at auction in 1883 for £460. During renovations an octagonal stone cistern, or creeing trough, was found in the original rear wall. It is similar to one in the north transept of St Andrew's Church.

Number 9, which once had a café in a shed, was, until the mid-1960s, the first dental surgery of Robert Waddell before he moved it initially to premises above the Co-op in St Helen's Street (page 27) and eventually to Princes Street. In 2007 the property, apart from the front wall, was demolished and rebuilt using, in part, glass brought from Sweden.

Number 2, next to the Market Place, is a hairdresser. Between it and number 4 is a door that leads to a rear yard.

Number 6, also double-fronted, was where a Roman altar and part of a Saxon cross were found under a house that was demolished in 1886 – the date above the door of the present property.

Above: Front Street from the bridge c.1900 and (right) the same view as it is today.

Numbers 8 and 10 have, above a common door lintel, the date *'R L 1707'* and the inscription *'Omnia Bona Bonis'* which can approximately be translated as *'To the good, all things are good'*. Number 10, **Oswald Cottage** ⑤⑧, has on its lintel, which was heightened in the early 19th century, the marriage mark *'RMB 1752'* (no-one has been able suggest whose initials these were).

Numbers 12, 14 and 16 are part of an incorporated terrace of three houses dating from about 1880. Numbers 14 and 16 are symmetrical with hood-moulded windows, ornamental finials and a rose window (page 11). The doorway between these two properties gives access to a communal rear yard for the three houses.

Opposite is the original shop front and the old wooden lintel of, initially, the Gallons' fish and chip shop and, later, Jean Hickleton's wool shop.

Number 18 used to be The Boot and Shoe public house, one of eight in Corbridge in 1824. The building dates, according to Pevsner, from the early 18th century. It was also, at one time, an old posting inn with stables behind. It was altered in the 1970s, but retained its symmetrical windows. Since then it has been a fish and chip shop, the first location of The Ramblers, an Italian and now a Chinese restaurant.

Number 26 has a long wooden lintel over its windows. It was the home of Robert Forster (see numbers 1 Front Street and 25 Middle Street) who was the local clockmaker – he added the minute hand to the church clock in 1861. He was also a historian – his *'History of Corbridge'* was published in 1881.

Number 28, **Narrowgate House** ⑤⑨, is named after the Narrowgate (now St Mary's Chare or more commonly Bad Bank) which falls steeply to the bridge just opposite. It has a symmetrical elevation with a projecting centre section and decorated finials.

Numbers 30, 32 and 34 were three cottages built to accommodate the employees of J. Jameson and Son, Corbridge Firebrick and Sanitary Tube Works, which was located on the northern outskirts of the village (page 17). The terrace was constructed by Davison, a local builder whose yard was opposite on the south side of the street and one of whose grandsons now owns the Orchard House Caravan Park (page 46) and another grandson the Dyvels Pine Furniture shop (page 47). Davison placed an advert in an Official Village Guide of the 1930s which responded to Hodgson's adverse picture of Corbridge in 1830 (page 8). It read *'Davison's, Builders, who have been for many years in business in the village, have done their part in altering the above dismal picture of the place. Fine stone-built dwellings on every land are eloquent testimony to their skill, and future historians will have something different to pen than Hodgson did a hundred years ago'*.

Above left: Oswald Cottage.

Above: Numbers 14 and 16 Front Street.

Left: South side of Front Street, looking east.

ST MARY'S CHARE

The steep cobbled lane leading down from Front Street is called St Mary's Chare and is a relic of the 13th century (page 9). Its name derives from the time when a path led from the village down to the Chapel of St Mary the Virgin. The passage is typical of old Corbridge with its paved path, rubble and coped walls, dressed quoins and finials, stone buildings and brick chimneys. The three cottages nearest to the river were built in 1877. To many local people the lane is known as Bad Bank which is probably a purely descriptive term.

The low stone building with the pantile roof (now an artefact shop) was **Bridge End Forge** 60, one of five smithies in Corbridge in 1885 and one of two owned by the Knott family. Known as 'Knott's Smithy', it was run by the same family for over 200 years and remained working until the mid 1970s.

The chapel of St Mary the Virgin stood at the northern end of the 13th century bridge. Later, and adjacent to it, was the Brigs-bar tollgate which was granted by deed in 1372. The name of the tollgate was still in use in 1632 though both the bridge and chapel had long since fallen into disrepair. In 1674, when the present bridge was built, a new tollhouse was erected at the foot of St Mary's Chare. Tolls were still being collected in 1881.

Right: Looking down and up St Mary's Chare (Bad Bank).

Below: What used to be 'Knott's Smithy'.

THE BRIDGE OVER THE TYNE

> **CORBRIDGE BRIDGE**
>
> THE FIRST MEDIEVAL BRIDGE BUILT IN 1235 REPLACED THE FORD AND FERRY BUT BECAME RUINOUS AND DANGEROUS IN THE 17TH CENTURY OWING TO FREQUENT FLOODS. THIS PRESENT SEVEN-ARCHED BRIDGE WAS COMPLETED IN 1674 AND IS THE SOLE BRIDGE FROM SOURCE TO MOUTH OF THE TYNE TO REMAIN STANDING AFTER THE SEVERE FLOOD OF 1771. ORIGINALLY BUILT FOR PACK-HORSE AND COACH TRAFFIC, IT WAS WIDENED IN 1881.

The bridge 61

The present bridge, with its seven unequal arches and voussoir stones, was built in 1674. It stands a few yards downstream from the one that was built in 1235 and destroyed 61 years later by William Wallace. During that period of 378 years, the only way to cross the river was by the ford located downstream from the present bridge (page 39). As described on a plaque at its southern end, this was the only bridge over the Tyne to survive the 1771 flood. Apparently the river was so high on that occasion that people on the bridge could lean over and wash their hands in it. Up to 1829, when the southernmost arch was rebuilt after a flood, there were steps up to the bridge on the south side making it unusable for horse and cart. A marker, indicating the river's depth, can be seen under the adjacent arch as can the original gas lamps on the bridge itself. The bridge was cantilevered and widened in 1881. When the bridge was built, a sundial was placed halfway across on the eastern parapet. This was replaced by a modern imitation by the County Council in 1981 when, as they were removing a temporary steel bridge which had been in use since 1971, the original was reputedly lost in the river. In 1992, when the water authority was laying a new pipe under the bridge, the foundations of the 1235 bridge were uncovered.

Diversion – south bank of the Tyne, the old Roman bridge and the Devil's Water

The embankment to the south of the river was first built in the 1870s in an attempt to reduce flooding, especially along Station Road. It was heightened after the 1955 flood (page 47) and then made wider and reinforced with imported clay, compacted by a heavy roller, in 2005. A pleasant walk along the Plantation, either along this embankment or beside the river itself, leads, after half a mile, to the approach to the old Roman bridge. Even in the early 19th century two or three stepped bases, each supporting short pillars, could be seen at low water until they were removed by the Greenwich Hospital Estates in 1833. In 2004, about 300 shaped stones from the former abutment were excavated from the river and, in 2007, used to recreate a replica ramp. The present site is 400 yards east of the Roman bridge as here the river-bank is not being eroded and impact on the flood-bank should be minimised. Shortly beyond is the confluence of the Devil's Water and the Tyne. DEFRA have created new permissive footpaths giving the option of a round walk with a sign-posted route back across the fields of the flood plain.

Above: An engraving of the bridge c.1882.

Below: The river bridge and Corbridge from the south-west.

The Boat House, the small building at the south-eastern end of the bridge, was built between the publication of the 1863 and 1895 OS maps. Despite its name there is no evidence that it was ever used as such.

Lion Court 62, opposite the car park and next to the roundabout at the northern end of Station Road, was known at the time of the 1891 census as Ealsfield House, a name derived from The Eals or Eals Field which was the whole area enclosed in 1304 and lying between Station Road, the river and The Stanners. Between 1930 and 1969 it was a maternity home, from which six mothers and their newly born babies had to be rescued during the 1955 flood. In 1969 it became the Lion of Corbridge Hotel and is now a block of luxury flats. A plaque shows the Corbridge crest surrounded by *'Sigill (um) Commune Corbridgie'*, i.e. 'The Seal of Corbridge' (page 29).

Right: Lion Court.

Diversion – The Stanners

This side-road, originally known as *'Holepethe'* (Hole Path), led to the ford which was used, mainly between 1296 and 1674 when there was no road bridge, by drovers to drive their cattle across the river to the foot of Spoutwell Lane on the north bank (page 39). Holpeth House is probably a corruption of 'Hole Path'.

The caravan park used to be the orchard of **Orchard House** (named Burncroft on the 1924 map). It subsequently became 'The Orchard Pleasure Park and Tea Gardens' which, together with a large building on the site, was used for major social events. It had, according to an official village guide of the mid-1930s, *'numerous facilities for recreation and in addition a maze, airy tea-rooms and a dance hall. Adequate accommodation in the case of unpropitious weather is also available'.* The building is still standing.

An advert in the same guide claims: *'Since it opened, The Orchard has been the means of bringing thousands of people to the village. The local papers say it is the most popular place for a day's outing on Tyneside.'*

Stanners Close, despite its Victorian appearance, is one of several stone-built houses erected here in 1906.

Station Road continued

The eight large Victorian houses, constructed by a builder called Burns who lived at Orchard House, form the so-called 'A to H terrace' (locally referred to as the ABC or alphabet houses) as their names begin, in order, with the first eight letters of the alphabet.

Tinklers Bank Foot 63 is the present name of what was a farm marked on 18th century maps and which at times has been known as Orchard House and Burncroft. Built of Ladycross stone (the quarry that supplied the stone is 5 miles south-west of Corbridge and is now also a nature reserve), it may be the house in the foreground on an 1834 etching called 'Corbridge on Tyne'. The 1841 census

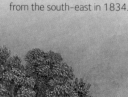

Below: Etching of Corbridge from the south-east in 1834.

Left: Station Road submerged in the 2005 flood.

lists two families, Davison and Richley, living here. A descendant of the former now owns the pine-furniture shop and, until 2004, the Dyvels.

Tinklers Bank Well, located in a field on a rise to the south of the station and belonging to the vicar of Corbridge, was also known as Priest's Well. It was open to everyone and it supplied Orchard House.

Station Road has been badly flooded three times in the last 50 years, in 1955, 1995 and 2005, the last two incidents resulting from the breaching of the flood protection bank (page 45).

The Dyvels 64, formerly the Station Inn (1863 OS map) or Hotel (1924 OS map), was flooded to a depth of 5 feet in 2005. During the 1995 flood, the then owner of the Dyvels caught a trout swimming outside his property, which he displayed in a sink as evidence. His wife, when rescued by boat in the 2005 flood, was told to *'sit tight as Station Road is quite choppy'*.

On the left is Tynedale Rugby Club and the site of the annual Northumberland County Show which attracts over 20,000 visitors on the Spring holiday Monday at the end of May.

Corbridge Station 65. The railway between Newcastle and Hexham was opened in 1835 and extended to Carlisle three years later. The railway was one of the first in the world to be used by passengers. The station, initially only on the south side of the line, was built in 1843 and the adjacent bridge

over the railway in 1847. According to Pevsner, the platform canopy is *'supported by Tuscan columns of cast iron'*. The station and the Station Master's House was a combined building and is now the Valley restaurant. At one time there was a 'firebrick and retort manufactory' near the station as well as, on the south side, the gas and sewage works. The abandoned arches under the road were part of the railway goods yard that remained in use until the 1960s.

Below: Looking towards Corbridge railway station and the Valley restaurant.

INDEX

For houses that have a number and no name, e.g. 14 Hill Street, look under the street name.